The new work that Larry Crane is teaching is a major break-through in the field of human behavior. One can eliminate all of their 'I can'ts' and transform them into 'I can's.' I highly recommend it to anyone who wants to overcome their limitations and become abundant with ease.

Dr. John L. Kemeny,
Albert Einstein Associate

The
Abundance
Book

by Lawrence Crane and Lester Levenson

The Easy Way to Riches, Health and Happiness
A Practical Way to Have it All

*If a mind
cannot
achieve peace
and quiet
it is unlikely
to achieve
anything else.*

*Dedicated to the best friend
anyone ever had.
The man who opened my eyes
to the truth — dear Lester.*

*With Love,
Larry*

The publishers and author of this material make no medical claim for its use.
This material is not intended to treat, diagnose, or cure any illness.
If you need medical attention, please consult with your medical practitioner.

CONTENTS

FOREWORD

By Dr. John L. Kemeny,
Albert Einstein Associate

I am 86 years old and I have been a research scientist, a surgeon, and a professor of psychiatry at Columbia University Medical School and at UCLA University Stress Center. I have also been a private consultant to Fortune 500 companies for over 60 years. I worked with Albert Einstein in my formative years.

In 1977, I met a physicist named Lester Levenson who discovered a profound breakthrough in the history of behavioral science. He liberated the subconscious mind and designed a simple method: How to get rid of negativity at any level. The method is called "The RELEASE® Technique". Lester Levenson and Larry Crane introduced me to and taught me this technique. I have practiced it for over 20 years myself successfully.

The new work that Larry Crane is teaching is a major step in facilitating the application of the Technique. By participating and experiencing this method, you will reach a place where nothing and no one will ever bother you again. A place where you can eliminate all your "I can't"s and replace them with "I can's". In order to get the full benefit of this course, I recommend that you participate experientially and follow the step-by-step exercises and instructions in this book exactly. I wish you a remarkable and joyful experience.

HOW THIS BOOK WILL HELP YOU

The Release® Technique (Releasing) is a powerful, unique and yet very practical tool that can significantly improve the quality and effectiveness of your life. This innovative method of self inquiry can assist you in experiencing whatever you believe your life should hold: more money, better relationships, physical well-being, improved career success or a renewed sense of meaning and purpose.

This may sound like a lot to promise, but we assure you it is not. The Release Technique is a life-transforming technique and yet it is easy to use. It is an innovative, original system that has been scientifically tested by leading doctors and researchers at some of the best universities in the country, and yet it is based on some of the world's most ancient and treasured secrets.

The Technique has been scientifically verified by Harvard, Columbia and State University of New York researchers. Researchers Dr. David McClelland of Harvard University and Dr. Richard Davidson of the State University of New York have found that "The Release Technique stands out far beyond the rest for its simplicity, efficiency, absence of questionable concepts and rapidity of results."

These studies also revealed that individuals using the technique show significant reduction in heart rate and diastolic blood pressure. With respect to short- versus long-term gain, the overall findings suggest that it is effective in promoting and maintaining stress reduction months after the training.

Researched by Albert Einstein Associate

Practicing psychiatrist, John L. Kemeny, M.D. and a former associate of Albert Einstein, said "I studied Larry's Releasing Technique. It was an enriching and enlightening experience. It provided new energy, spontaneity and fresh insights. I wholeheartedly recommend this program to anyone interested in improving their life."

Until recently, The Release Technique was only available to a small number of people through private classes. However, after years of experimentation we have found new ways to effectively introduce it in different forms. So we can now invite you to participate in one of life's truly remarkable and empowering adventures--the journey of self-inquiry and self-mastery.

How can you be sure that the time you spend learning and using this technique will allow you to create the kinds of changes you desire in your life? The answer is simple. The Release Technique is not just a set of ideas and theories. It is practical technology that you can begin working with today to produce direct and measurable results in your life.

The Release Technique is so effective because it works directly on you as the primary instrument of change. It does not deal with effects. It deals with cause. It does not promise you strategies that will change the outside environment. And it certainly does not suggest that you use manipulation, no matter how subtly, to change someone else's behavior. Instead, it echoes the very sound and practical suggestion of noted psychologist Carl Jung, who said "If things go wrong in the world, something is wrong in me. Therefore, if I am sensible, I shall but myself right first."

Is it the things going on around you that are causing distress; or is it your reaction to them?

The byproduct of this internal change though is a massively noticeable change of the outside environment. Energy begets like energy--once you change your inner being people and circumstances change accordingly. These changes are tangible and instantly provable. As Lester Levenson said repeatedly in his scientifically pragmatic way: "Don't believe anything I say, take it for checking."

AUTHOR'S NOTE

"The only method of receiving love is to give love,
because what we give out must come back."
--Lester Levenson

ABOUT LESTER LEVENSON AND HOW
THE RELEASE TECHNIQUE WAS BORN

Lester Levenson was born in Elizabeth, New Jersey, on July 19, 1909, to Jewish emigrant parents. He grew up much loved, doted on by his parents and three sisters. Yet his predominant characteristic was shyness. He was extremely withdrawn and introspective, constantly wondering what this life was about. His parents were not really religious but his grandfathers on both sides were holy people, rabbis. Lester was 21 when his beloved mother and father died. He refused to say the prayer for the dead. "Will that bring them back? If it does, I'll say it." Then defiantly he turned away from God.

Lester sailed through school and college with astonishing ease, becoming a physicist, an engineer, a successful businessman and a self-made millionaire. Yet despite all his achievements there was an innate turmoil in his heart, an anxiety and stress that seemed to rule his life.

In 1952, at the age of 42, Lester had his second massive heart attack. In those days, they did not have bypass surgery or heart transplants and so when he came out of the emergency room, the doctors told him, "Lester, we're sorry to tell you, but you have two weeks to live, three at the most, and we can't do anything for you. So we're sending you home."

So Lester went home.

He was extremely fearful of dying, but he said to himself, "You're still breathing, Lester; there is still a chance." Then he sat down and began thinking around-the-clock. He had always been considered a brilliant man. Always on the honor roll. The recipient of a four-year scholarship to Rutgers University back in the days when few scholarships were handed out. But he said to himself, "Lester, you are stupid, stupid, stupid! All this accumulated knowledge, all this intellect has gotten you to the place that you're a dead man! And if you don't uncover what's in the way, eliminate it, you're going to die!"

Being a physicist, he knew he had to go back to the drawing board, wipe the slate clean, and start from point zero. So he started to examine his life. He noticed that each time he was ill he was wanting something and that the intense wanting feelings were what was actually making him miserable. He wanted love, he wanted money, he wanted to change things, and every time he looked at that wanting, he had an uncomfortable feeling that he traced back to his illness. Then he noticed that whenever he was giving and loving and wasn't wanting anything, he was not ill. So, he asked himself, "Well, if I could get rid of all my non-loving feelings, would I get better?" He thought about this question and uncovered something that was startling to him at the time.

He noticed that when he was loving he was happiest. That happiness equated to being *loving* rather than being *loved*.

> *HE NOTICED THAT WHEN HE WAS LOVING HE WAS HAPPIEST. THAT HAPPINESS EQUATED TO BEING LOVING RATHER THAN TO BEING LOVED.*

That was a starting point. He asked himself if he could cure his illnesses this way. So, he began connecting all of his thoughts and feelings in that direction--from that of "wanting to be loved", to that of "loving". He examined all his relationships and he let go of all of his non-loving feelings from the past. In that process he made another shocking discovery: He saw that he wanted to change the entire world and that was the cause of all his ailments, making him a slave to this world. He decided to reverse that by actually unloading the subconscious concepts and pressures and by taking responsibility for everything happening in his life. At this point he discovered that limitations were only concepts in our minds and can easily be dropped. He realized that God is within us all, that we are infinite beings with no limitations. With that realization, he became happier: freer, lighter and with an overall sense of well-being.

Later on he would say: "We are all gods acting like goddamned fools."

Months went by and Lester still wasn't dead. He hardly went to sleep, he ate a little bit, and he continued to work on himself. He corrected his physical body. All of his miseries dropped away and he found himself in a place in which he was happy all the time, without sorrow. He totally cured himself.

More than that, Lester unlocked the science of the mind: How the mind works, what to do about it and how to correct it. How to correct your thinking. How to call up the menu of your mind, take a look at this menu and eliminate what you don't want.

Lester was a giving person--one thousand percent! He spent the remainder of his life helping others discover this secret that he had unlocked for himself.

He passed on in 1994 at the age of 84--42 years after being told he had two to three weeks to live!

And before he died, he asked me to continue his work.

Larry Crane
June 2002

INTRODUCTION

WE BEGIN

"You should not believe anything we say, but prove it out for yourself by having great wealth, happiness, well being and health in your life."
--Lester Levenson

My name is Larry Crane and I welcome you to the Abundance Course. Abundance does not just mean money: It means health, it means wealth, it means everything in life--an abundance of everything. I will be guiding you through a series of incredible techniques--very simple, very profound--that will allow you to eliminate anything that stands in the way of you having total abundance in your life. It is easily in my opinion the most amazing discovery in the history of mankind.

> **"WE ARE UNLIMITED BEINGS— LIMITED ONLY BY THE CONCEPTS OF LIMITATION WE HOLD IN OUR MINDS."**

The book EMOTIONAL INTELLIGENCE by Daniel Goleman recently spent time as the #1 bestseller on the New York Times   list. The premise of the book is that our emotional intelligence is much more important in predicting our level of success and satisfaction in life than our I.Q. In fact, the book has redefined what it means to be smart and effective in life.

In his book, Goleman defines five critical skills that make up emotional intelligence. The following is a summation of these skills and how they relate to the Abundance Course and the skill of releasing.

#1. Knowing one's emotions. Self-awareness--recognizing a feeling as it happens--is the keystone of emotional intelligence. The ability to monitor what we are feeling moment to moment is crucial to psychological insight and self understanding. The course is designed to help you gain better awareness of what you are feeling moment to moment. There are also specific exercises in the course that will give you a roadmap to your emotions and effective tools to deal with them. New research is discovering that being aware of our emotions helps us to make better decisions and inappropriate emotional responses cloud our judgment. The course includes specific processes that will help you to eliminate the inappropriate emotional responses that cause you to make decisions that you later regret.

#2. Managing emotions. Handling feelings so they are appropriate. "The RELEASE® Technique" goes beyond managing your emotions by giving you a powerful tool to let go of or eliminate the painful and limiting emotions and stress that prevent you from performing at your best and being able to bounce back from life's inevitable setbacks and challenges. It also will show you how to eliminate the emotional baggage and patterns that stem from the traumas and disappointments of the past.

#3. Motivating oneself. Marshaling emotions in service to a goal is essential for paying attention, for self-motivations and mastery and for creativity. Emotional self-control --delaying gratification and stifling impulsiveness--underlies accomplishment of every sort. And being able to get into the "flow" state enables outstanding performance of all kinds. The tools you will learn in our basic course will show you how to easily eliminate the blocking feelings that prevent you from achieving what you want in life. As you eliminate the feelings that say, "I can't! I don't know how! I don't deserve it! I can't handle it!" you uncover your innate sense of "I can" that naturally catapults you to greater success. Our inappropriate emotions cause us to act impulsively. As you let them go, you find it easier to stick with your goals. Graduates report that consistent use of the method results in greater access to the "flow" state. The course will also show you specific processes designed to help you achieve all you desire.

#4. Recognizing emotions in others. Empathy is the fundamental people skill. As you use the technique, you will not only become more aware of your own emotions, you will be able to recognize the emotions of others and attune yourself to their needs and wants.

#5. Handling relationships. The art of relationship is, in a large part, skill in managing emotions in others. As you let go of your own emotional baggage and increase your empathy by releasing, you naturally develop an ability to relate better to others. As you learn that you are a master of your emotions, you intuitively know how to guide others toward their own emotional mastery. Also, as you use "The RELEASE® Technique" and let go of your own emotional baggage, people will enjoy relating to you and giving you what you want.

Now, let me tell you about myself. I was born in the Bronx. I grew up in a poor family. We never missed a meal, but I thought the rich man lived on the top floor and the poor man lived in the basement. And we lived in the basement. As a young boy, I had many, many jobs; I was very aggressive. I worked hard, put myself through New York University, The Leonard Stern School of Business, and when I graduated college in 1957, my father told me if I could make $100 a week, it would be a terrific accomplishment. I noticed some of my friends who graduated started to be successful and were making lots of money, so I said to myself, "I'm just as smart as they are. I can do that, too." So I went about life and business in a very aggressive way, like "Get outta my way--I'll take what I want--I'm gonna have what I want or I'll knock you down." And in time, I climbed my way to the top.

During that period I got married and had twin sons but never made any time for them. I started in the advertising business and quickly became the advertising and marketing director of Remco Toys. After a few very successful years, I started my own direct mail business, Telehouse, Inc., which was the first of its kind to sell record packages on television. The company quickly became very successful. We started to make millions of dollars. I divorced my first wife and married a beautiful, beautiful woman. I bought a ten-room duplex penthouse in Manhattan. I had the limousines, the planes--I had businesses all over the world making multi-millions. Yet, I was absolutely miserable!

It was quite confusing to me. One night I came home to my fabulous ten-room Manhattan penthouse apartment. Time magazine had written an article about me, and the doorman greeted me with, "Mr. Crane, what an honor to have you in my building. For me to take you up to your penthouse is my pleasure." This was a Friday night around 9 p.m. and I remember getting out of the elevator and being so unhappy and so miserable that I actually walked over to the terrace and for about two hours I contemplated jumping--ending it all. I call this the second greatest day of my life! (The first: learning "The RELEASE® Technique" from Lester.) But that Friday evening I, too, examined my life. I asked myself what am I doing on the planet? What is life about? I observed that I did not know what I was doing on Earth, but for me life was only about making money. I was so focused on money that I did not even allow myself to spend much, enjoy much or do much with it. That was confusing. I decided that evening to find an answer. After all, I had no reason to be miserable: I had millions of dollars, a beautiful wife, a fabulous business, businesses all over the world, media attention, and so on and so forth. Still, I was miserable. I was not interested in drugs or drinking. These things had no appeal to me and thank God I never turned in that direction. Since I was not willing to jump and end it, I needed to find an answer.

At the time, I was not receptive to psychiatric work. I was not open to transcendental meditation or yoga. I was pretty closed in those days and yet I wasn't willing to jump. So I became determined to find an answer. What that answer was, I did not know. My wife at the time talked me into some New Age courses, which I took, but I still found no answer after taking a number of them and trying to put an end to my unhappiness. I tried and tried, but I did not have the answer that I wanted. All I really wanted was to get out of my misery. I discovered I was angry. I discovered I had fear. I discovered I was doing things that were destructive and not quite intelligent behavior, yet I didn't know what to do about it. None of the courses showed me what to do about it. I just became more and more frustrated. I then took some additional courses, but still to no avail.

Then one day, in 1976, a man came into my office to sell me a mail order item. I had some interesting spiritual or self-discipline quotations on my office wall which often opened up a conversation of what I was into and the answers I was seeking. This salesman told me about "The RELEASE® Technique". It really resonated with me, so I decided to take the course that very weekend. That same weekend, I met a man called Lester Levenson, my mentor, my teacher, who I was fortunate enough to know for twenty-two years. I spoke to him almost every day, many times during the day. I took trips with him around the country and was quite fascinated by his clarity, his calmness and his givingness. He, too, was a multi-millionaire, but didn't seem to work hard at all. In fact, early in our relationship he said, "One should never believe a word I say."

And I say that to all those reading this book: "Don't believe a word I say, but take it for checking."

These are the words that Lester told me. Take it for checking. Everything that I'm going to present to you is provable if you take a chance and prove it and demonstrate it yourself. I will discuss some things you may consider "far out," but if you take it for checking, you'll discover your own truth as I did.

No one can be taught truth, each must realize truth by himself. A teacher can give direction and the pupil may take it. All truth is provable. Accept nothing on hearsay. Each must prove everything for himself.

I ONLY KNOW WHAT I CAN DO, NOT SAY. PROVE IT. The first thing Lester told me was: "There is no such thing as a germ." Wow! That was a tremendous statement because in those days I'd catch colds by just talking on the phone with a sniffler. I had it all: ulcers, migraine headaches. I used to scream at the top of my lungs ten times a day (a sure candidate for a heart attack), and I had all the illnesses to go along with that state, including rose fever, hay fever, and every allergy known to man. So I decided to use "The RELEASE® Technique" on those very illnesses.

Then one day Lester informed that working was not the ultimate thing to do. I said: "What?"(At the time, I was working seven days a week, sixteen hours a day. I was making lots of money, but I was very unhappy and very confused about it.) He said, "If hard work had anything to do with making money, a ditch digger should be rich!" Well, that kind of made sense, but what then should one do? He showed me some special techniques and gave me some "releasing" assignments to do by myself. Lester called this his "Butt" system: You sit at home on your butt and just by letting go of your limiting thoughts and feelings, great things happen. That was a radical idea, but since I had confidence in Lester and I had proved to myself that the Release Technique had worked on my illnesses, I decided to try it with regard to my company. I found even greater success. I discovered by using these simple techniques that I could get richer, more successful, happier, healthier, wiser, work easier, and have abundance in my life with ease and simplicity.

What I am about to show you is just how to do that yourself. It is easy. It is possible and anybody can do it. We have even taught this course to 5-year-olds and they use it successfully. Why? Because we all have a natural ability to let go. In the following pages, I am going to show you just how to do it. First, we are going to kind of walk around a little bit. Perhaps I will discuss something that might feel a little uncomfortable to you, but if you release and check it out, you will see the clarity of my illustration. Once again, "Don't believe a word I'm saying--take it for checking." Experience is the best way to learn.

I will guide you through this experience and give you everything that Lester gave me. By using this technique, you will have unlimited abundance, you will work easier and smarter, illnesses will disappear, relationships will get better. Everything in your world will just improve. It's that simple. So relax, sit back and we will continue.

Now let's talk about what people are looking for--what everyone is looking for--and how to get it.

Everyone is looking for "happiness with no sorrow" or peace of mind, but most people are looking for this outside themselves. They are looking for it in someone, in some thing, in making money, being a big shot, having possessions. Unfortunately, it is impossible to find peace of mind that way. Take it for checking. Take a look at somebody who is powerful, who is monetarily successful. How happy are they? How satisfied are they? Do they really have peace of mind?

Let's take a look at those individuals who are trying to get happiness and peace of mind from a relationship. Does that relationship give peace of mind? Take a check and see if you have happiness with no sorrow, peace of mind, and where you are looking for it. Are you seeking it in a person who is unhappy or relatively unhappy? You must go inside yourself in order to find peace of mind and happiness. By unloading your limitations, you will discover that you are already unlimited and you can do anything you want. Just unload your limiting thoughts.

Peace of mind means a quiet mind, not a noisy mind. That is why only a few of us ever find it. We are looking for peace of mind outside ourselves and peace of mind can only be acquired by having a quiet mind. The more one quiets his or her mind, the more powerful one becomes. That is what we are going to explore. You will learn how to accomplish this yourself.

Until recently, The Release Technique was only available to people by word of mouth and in small groups. About forty thousand people have learned this technique. I started teaching this course after Lester taught me his famous "Butt" system, the method of sitting on one's butt and getting everything one wants by simply "releasing." A way of examining one's subconscious mind, calling up the menu of the subconscious mind and knocking it out. In no way is this analytical. I am not going to motivate you nor will I pump you with wonderful slogans. I will merely show you how releasing is done and gently guide you through it the same way Lester taught me. Remember, YOU must experience it in order to benefit from it.

If you read this material intellectually, you will not get much out of it. However, if you actually do the exercises and experience releasing, you will discover the most amazing, earth-shattering treasure in the history of mankind: A way to unlock your subconscious mind, call up the menu of your mind, examine what you don't want and knock it out--totally eliminate it. It is that simple, yet that profound! Once again, analysis is unnecessary. This method does not require analyzing past negative experiences. After all, if I have a splinter in my finger, I really don't care how I got it, why I got it, how big it is, what color it is or who gave it to me. I simply want to take tweezers and pull it out! The Release Technique allows you this simplicity.

CHAPTER ONE

THE RELEASE TECHNIQUE
And its profound effects on every aspect of life

Unique Features of The Release Technique

1. The Release Technique is the only technique that enables you to eliminate stress at its source--as you feel it--as opposed to trying to manage, avoid or cope with the symptoms and effects of stress.

2. This technique is self-empowering and helps you to become self-sufficient by avoiding dependent relationships on counselors, trainers or other outside authorities.

3. The Release Technique works anywhere, any time on any issue in your personal or professional life.

4. Results increase over time. The effect of eliminating stress is cumulative. The more you use this method the greater your ability to make positive changes in behavior and to handle difficult situations with greater ease.

5.This exciting enlightening course will help you:
*Rid yourself of fear, which is holding you back from having everything in life.
*Rid yourself of failure habits that hold you back in life, such as procrastination.
*Find out just what satisfaction is and how to get it.
*Feel love any time you want it--with ease.
*Learn how to trust yourself.
*Rid yourself of worrying and spinning.
*Access answers from your higher self, instead of being frustrated with old answers or no answers.
*Rid yourself of the habit of beating yourself up.
*Clear away the years of accumulated confusion.
*Have abundant health, joy and riches.
*Be in total control of your life with ease.

The Release Technique is unique. It is not a compilation or takeoff on any other course or technique. Because of this it will not duplicate any other training program or personal development work.

If you have any difficulty along the way, please feel free to call our releasing hot line at 818-385-0611, Monday through Friday, 9am to 5pm, Pacific Standard Time.

I have taught the Abundance Course to executives of Fortune 500 companies for years. I have personally trained doctors, psychiatrists, sports and entertainment celebrities, sales people, managers, and housewives in the art of letting go of problems, unwanted emotions and all forms of stress. I call it Releasing.

Dr. David Hawkins, known as the Father of Orthomolecular Psychiatry, who published a textbook on the subject with Nobel prize winner Linus Pauling, conducted scientific studies on The Release Technique. He states: "The Release Technique is more effective than the other approaches currently available to relieving the physiologic responses to stress. In my researches of all the various stress reduction and consciousness programs, The Release Technique stood out far and beyond the rest for its sheer simplicity, efficiency, absence of questionable concepts and rapidity of observable results. Its simplicity is deceptive and almost disguises the real power of the technique."

Simply stated, this technique releases emotional attachments and aversions. Use of the technique proves the observation made by every sage for thousands of years: That attachments and aversions are the cause of all suffering on every level. The mind, with its thoughts, is driven by feelings. Each feeling is the cumulative derivative of many thousands of thoughts. Because most people throughout their lives repress, suppress and seek to escape their feelings, the suppressed energy accumulates and seeks expression through psychosomatic distress, bodily disorders, emotional illnesses and disordered behavior in interpersonal relationships. The accumulated feelings can cause illness as well as blocking success in all areas of life.

The benefits of The Release Technique can, therefore, be described on various levels.

Physical
The release of the suppressed emotions results in decrease of the overflow of energy into the body's autonomic nervous system and unblocks the acupuncture energy system (the later can be demonstrated by kinesiology). Therefore, as a person constantly releases, physical and psychosomatic disorders improve and frequently ultimately disappear altogether. There is a general reversal of pathologic processes in the body and a return to optimum functioning.

Behavioral
Because there is a progressive decrease of anxiety and negative emotions, there is less and less need for escapism via drugs, alcohol, entertainment or excessive sleeping. Consequently, there is an increase in vitality, energy and sense of well-being and more efficient and effortless functioning in all areas.

Interpersonal Relationships

As negative feelings are released, there is a progressive increase of positive feelings which results in quickly observable improvement in all relationships, with the increase in the capacity to love. Conflicts with others decrease progressively, so that job performance improves. The elimination of negative blocks allows vocational goals to be more easily accomplished, and self-sabotaging behavior based on guilt progressively diminishes. There is less and less dependence on intellectualism and greater use of intuitive knowingness. There is often the uncovering of previously unsuspected creative and psychic abilities with the resumption of personality growth and development which in all people is thwarted by suppressed negative emotions. Of greater importance is the progressive diminution of dependency, that bane of all human relationships, which underlies so much pain and suffering up to and including violence and suicide as its ultimate expression. There is also a diminution of aggressiveness and hostile behavior and its replacement with feelings of acceptance and lovingness toward others.

Emotional Growth

The most obvious and visible effect of releasing is a resumption of emotional and psychological growth and the solving of problems which often have been of long standing. There is pleasure and satisfaction as one begins to experience the powerful effects of releasing blocks to achievement and satisfaction. It is soon discovered that limitations, negative beliefs and many thoughts that had naively been held to be true were all merely the accumulated negative feelings. When the feeling is let go, the thought pattern changes from "I can't" to "I can."

The rate of emotional growth which graduates of the Course report is related to the consistency with which they release their negative feelings. And there is no relationship to age. Students have ranged in age from the teens to the nineties with equal benefit. Repressed feelings require a counter energy to keep them submerged. As these feelings are released, that energy is now freed for constructive uses. There is, therefore, an increase in available energy for creativity, growth, work and interpersonal relationships. The quality and enjoyment of these activities increase. Most people are too exhausted to bring really high quality into their experiences unless the negative programs opposing them have been resolved.

Problem Solving

The effectiveness of the method in problem solving often is quite astonishing. Understanding the process involved here is very important because it is quite different than the world's other methods. When you are released on the feeling behind the question, release on any other feelings that you might also be having about what seems to be the problem. When

DON'T LOOK FOR ANSWERS; INSTEAD LET GO OF THE FEELING BEHIND THE QUESTION.

you are finally fully released, the answer will be there waiting for you. You won't have to look for it. Consider how simple and easy this is compared to the mind's usual long drawn out inefficient attempts at problem solving. Usually the mind hunts and pecks endlessly, fumbling around with first this possible answer and then that one. The reason the mind can't decide is because it is looking in the wrong place.

This use of the method is also very rewarding in all decision making. When you first clear out the underlying feelings, the decisions are more realistic and wise. Think of how often you have changed your mind and regretted past decisions. That is because there was an unrecognized and unreleased feeling behind the decision. Then, when the action that was decided upon was taken, the underlying feeling shifts. Then, from the viewpoint of the new feeling space, the decision turns out to be a decision that you really did not want. This happens with such regularity that most people develop a fear of decision making.

Problem solving using the releasing method can often be lightning quick with problems of long standing. To discover how fast it can work, try it for yourself. Take several problems of long standing and stop looking for answers. Look to see what is the underlying feeling that produced the question in the first place. Once you let that go, the answer will present itself automatically.

Goal Setting and Achievement
An article about The Release Technique on this subject appeared in Brain/Mind Bulletin in August, 1982, entitled "Intense Wanting May Bar Getting." In it, the article stated: "Wanting to change something can be the primary impediment to change. Longing reinforces our sense of lack and strengthens feelings of neediness. Ironically, these feelings in turn prevent one from thinking clearly about how to achieve the desired outcome. The stress that results from this paradox may be released by a technique known as the Release Technique. This system concentrates specifically on releasing the frustrations and tensions associated with unmet expectations."

Lifestyle
You will notice that a lot of your activities, like your attachments and aversions, are based on fear and anger, guilt and pride. As these are released in any given area, you move up to courage. On that level, changes in your life begin to occur. Or, if you choose to continue the same activity, your motivation is different and therefore you will experience different results than you had been getting in the past. At the least, the emotional payoff will be different. Instead of grim satisfaction, you may experience joy. You may find yourself doing the thing now because you love it rather than because you have to. The energy requirement will certainly be much less.

One delightful discovery you will make is that your capacity for love is far beyond what you ever dreamt. The more you release the more loving you become. More and more of your life will be spent lovingly, doing things that you love to do with people for whom you feel increasing love. As this happens, your life becomes transformed. You look different. People respond differently to you. You are relaxed and happy. People are attracted to you. Waitresses and cab drivers suddenly, mysteriously become attentive and courteous and you will wonder "what's coming over this world, anyway?" (The answer to that one is "you are!") You are coming into your own power. It happens of its own. You are now influencing everyone with whom you come into contact in a favorable way. Love is the most powerful of the emotional energy vibrations. For love, people will go to any length and do things which they would never do for any amount of money.

There are literally thousands of examples that could be cited of the rapid expansions that take place in one's life when the "I can't"'s are released. On the other hand, life situations often of long standing may suddenly resolve themselves and this shift of balance may upset friends and family members because of the shift of balance. Things that have been done out of constriction, fear and guilt or a sense of duty may suddenly be thrown overboard. New levels of consciousness change perception and new horizons open up. Many motives which drive people may suddenly become meaningless. Money, position, prestige, power, ambition, competitiveness and the need for security may diminish, and are often replaced by the motivations of love, cooperation, fulfillment, freedom, creative expression, expansion of consciousness, understanding and spiritual awareness. There tends to be more reliance on intuition and feelings than on thinking, reason and logic. People who are very "yang" may discover their "yin" side and vice versa. Rigid patterns give way to flexibility. Safety becomes less important than discovery and exploration.

Paradoxically in this elevated state of consciousness, one experiences effortless attainment of any and all goals: relationships, position, money, health, and looks spontaneously improve to previously unimagined levels.

Personal lives pick up momentum, and movement replaces stuck-in-a-rut life patterns.

One surprising observation about the releasing method is that major changes can take place very rapidly. Lifetime patterns can suddenly disappear, long standing inhibitions can be let go of in a matter of minutes, hours, a day. Rapid changes are accompanied by an increased feeling of well-being, as well as the appearance of aliveness. The energy released by the letting go of negativity now flows into positive attitudes, thoughts and feelings so that there is a progressive increase of personal power. Thoughts are now more effective. More and more is accomplished with less and less effort. Intention is made powerful by the removal of doubts, fears and inhibitions and dynamic forces are therefore released so that what were once impossible dreams now become actualized goals.

Resolution of Psychological Problems--Comparison with Psychotherapy

In general, releasing is far more rapid than psychotherapy of any variety. It is also far more liberating and far more stimulating to growth of consciousness and awareness. Psychotherapy, however, is better designed to elucidate underlying patterns. Releasing greatly facilitates and speeds up psychotherapy and it also raises its goals. Psychotherapy is also more gratifying intellectually because of its verbal nature and its focus on the "whys" behind behavior. However, that is also its weakness. Too often intellectual insight is all that is really achieved and the emotional working through is slow and often painful and avoided. Releasing is concerned with the emotional "what" from moment to moment and it does not involve intellect. The "why" becomes apparent of itself once the "what" has been released.

Releasing has a domino effect in that releasing on one negative feeling also releases the energy behind all other negative feelings, so there is a constant across the board benefit. For instance, a successful educated man had a life-long fear of heights, an intense phobia. He had many pressing problems in his life so that after learning how to release he was very busy with letting go of his feelings and fears about life problems and never got around to specifically releasing on his life-long fear of heights. When he was later in a situation involving standing on a roof, he was amazed to discover that the fear had greatly lessened. He was amazed and delighted. To test his newfound freedom he first climbed up a ladder and he also got on the roof of a skyscraper for over an hour with no discomfort. This illustrates that as one fear is released all fear is diminished non-specifically.

The goal of releasing is the elimination of the very source of all suffering and pain. This sounds radical and startling and, in fact, it is! Ultimately all negative feelings stem from the ego. When enough negative feelings have been released, your true self is revealed. When the ego itself is released upon, the ego dissolves. The source of suffering, therefore, loses the very essence of its power.

Each of us has a certain amount of limitations, directly related to the amount of negative feelings we have stored up. When the pressure behind these feelings has been released, that emotion no longer occurs. For instance, if fear is constantly released for a period of time, eventually it runs out. It then becomes difficult or almost impossible to feel further fear. It takes progressively more and more stimuli to elicit it. Finally, a person who releases a great deal has to diligently search for fear. Anger also progressively diminishes so that even a major provocation fails to elicit anger. A person with little fear or anger primarily feels love all the time and experiences a loving acceptance of events and people and the vicissitudes of life.

The goal of releasing is to get to a place where you have abundance, where nothing and nobody can ever bother you again. Then you will forever be happy with no pain or sorrow. Psychotherapy accepts levels of behavior as healthy that, from the viewpoint of releasing, is quite unacceptable. For instance, in psychotherapy, fear, anger and pride might be considered to be acceptable states of functioning, but as we have seen, the innate destructiveness behind those states is really not necessary and they could more easily be eliminated by releasing--thus allowing one to become abundant.

My wish for everyone is that everyone attain the highest state possible so that here on earth we have that heaven that everyone dreams of, where life is beautiful, life is easy and everyone has the greatest love and respect for everyone else. This would cause all misery to drop away, all sickness to disappear, all thoughts of war and destructiveness to be eliminated from our minds and, in place of it, just the opposite: love, beauty and joy.

To sum up, my overall wish is for everyone to fully know what I know so that all misery and unhappiness may be at an end.

It is easy to show you how to have abundance because the ability to have abundance is already there, in you. Remember, thousands of people have already proven this. In fact, until recently, all the people that we have helped have come to us through word of mouth. Can you imagine thousands of people coming to you by word of mouth only?

After scientifically proving that this system works for everyone who learns it, my only wish is to have as many people as possible learn how to have abundance with ease. And you are about to join the thousands in having abundance for yourself. Welcome!

CHAPTER TWO

GETTING THE MOST FROM
THE ABUNDANCE COURSE

Scientific researchers who have studied "The Release® Technique" found out through working with thousands of people that the only effective way to create spectacular and instantaneous benefits is by actually DOING it. Reading about it will certainly appeal to you intellectually but only by using it experientially will you quickly realize the huge advantage of this practical method.

Why? Because giving you a lot of intellectually appealing materials won't help much at all. Why? Because the intellectual approach is *way too slow.* Lester found that out! He was widely read and had learned much in his life, but that didn't help him when the chips were down. No, what helped him was when he discovered and used this ability. And used it experientially. And quickly. And you can, too!

Furthermore, this should be your clue as to why some things you may have tried before just didn't work. Anyone attempting to recall this ability intellectually would spend decades trying to "make sense out of it," if it could be done at all. By using "The RELEASE® Technique", you will discover it, prove it, experience it for yourself, and begin to use it on the VERY FIRST DAY. Now.

Releasing is something you must experience. You won't learn to release unless you actually go through the releasing process yourself in a step-by-step fashion. To try to intellectually understand how to release by simply reading about it instead of doing it is the same as reading about swimming, but being unwilling to get into the water (or reading a book on how to ride a bicycle or trying to understand what chocolate tastes like, but being unwilling to eat it.) You SIMPLY MUST DO IT EXPERIENTIALLY, because it CANNOT be done intellectually. It must be read in a special way. You will need to become a participant and do the actual exercises in order to discover how it feels to release. After you do, you'll have the ability to create the unlimited life you deserve.

Having this book in your possession is like having an instructor at your beck and call; anytime you want an instructor's help, just turn to a particular page. Just sit back and watch your limitations fly away with minimal effort on your part--it's that simple. You'll have the opportunity to work on issues that are important to you and you'll learn more about the technique as I guide you through the experience, just as Lester taught me.

Do not forget, your firsthand experience is what counts--learn and experience it for yourself instead of being told about it--then it's yours forever. It's an exciting, experiential learning process.

Consider how it would be if you got rid of all your limitations. How would your life be if you had no limitations and you rid yourself of the limitations that are holding you back? If you got rid of your guilt? If you got rid of your fears? If you got rid of procrastination? If you got rid of beating yourself up? Any of these feelings can be released and you will be able to do this using the Release Technique. It is that simple. All I ask you to do is follow the bouncing ball--let me guide you through it gently just like Lester guided me through it and you will be happy and healthy and wealthy and wise.

So, I welcome you to the most adventurous, profound, incredible journey in the history of mankind. Welcome to the Abundance Course.

Before moving ahead to Chapter Three, please take a moment and write down your intentions for this course. Write what you hope to get out of this course (you can have more than one intention.) Use the following chart. It is very important to know just where you are going. It is like driving in unknown territory without a map: If you do not know where you are going, you cannot expect to get there! Most of us are confused and not aware of where we are going. We want you to be clear about your direction. Take a few moments and think about what your intentions are. And write them down. (Remember me talking about your participation? This is where you implement it: stop reading, and give yourself the gift of writing out your intentions right now.)

In order to get the maximum benefit from this course, follow it chapter by chapter. It is important to do the exercises in the exact order in which they are presented.

Start by getting a pencil right now, and writing your intentions for the course on the next page.

WRITE YOUR INTENTIONS FOR THE COURSE
(What you hope to accomplish)

Here is an opportunity to focus on the issues that are most important to you. View this sheet as a "wish list" of whatever you would like to change or improve in all areas of your life, both personally and professionally. You can refer back to this list from time to time to find issues you would like to address. This course is the beginning of many positive changes in your life, so allow your list to far exceed what you think you can accomplish during the course.

PERSONAL:

To worry less

To relax more without guilt

To be happier

To be more patient

To be more loving

Less anxious

Not to dwell on things I cant change

To hate less or not at all.

To drink less

PROFESSIONAL:

To have more time

Less work stress

Earn more money more easily

Build another business

Learn + pass IFA exams

Have constant good referrals

CHAPTER THREE

LET'S DELVE DEEPER

Love will give not only all the power in the universe,
it will give all the joy and all the knowledge
--Lester Levenson

Now we will begin to explore how to release, let go and eliminate whatever is bothering us.

The sound or voice that plays in your head? Sometimes it plays a nice sound and, sometimes, not such a nice sound. Ask yourself, "Whose voice is it?" Is it not your voice?

Since it is your voice, you must have programmed it. Therefore, you ought to be able to erase it. Why should you have to listen to something that drives you crazy? After eating a big meal, why should you find yourself moments later standing in front of a refrigerator eating again? Why should you feel like you have to "tell somebody off" when you know it is going to cause you big problems? Why should you get so agitated driving that you start chasing the car in front of you? Who said we have to do these things?

Unfortunately, emotions run us. There is a saying: "What's going around in the world is emotional sickness." It is when we become reactive that problems usually begin for us. So let us explore how to erase these negative thoughts and feelings (the "voices") that play in our head.

The unit that sits on our shoulders called the "head" is simply a recording and playback unit. Its only job is to record and play back whatever happens to us. If you should ask it to think about how to make a million dollars, it is going to play back everything you know about making a million dollars. If you ask it about your health situation, it is going to instantaneously play back all of the previous information you have collected over the years on health. Unfortunately, this unit also plays back other pre-recorded sounds and thoughts when you do not want to hear them, interfering with your concentration, sleep and peace of mind!

FOUR WAYS OF HANDLING A FEELING
In general, the world knows of three ways of handling a feeling. These ways are to suppress (hide) the feeling, express (vent) the feeling, or try to escape

(cope) from the feeling or situation.

We teach a fourth option for handling a feeling. This is "The RELEASE® Technique", which allows you to "let go" of the feeling to discharge any negative energy.

1.   SUPPRESS (Hide)
This is the most common and most harmful thing you can do with feelings. Pushing feelings down causes a build-up of repressed energy (stress), which eventually drives you to behave automatically in ways you don't like and wouldn't choose if you weren't being driven by the feelings. Suppressed feelings eventually take their toll on emotional and physical health.

2.   EXPRESS (Vent)
Expressing puts the feeling into action and sometimes gives you a short-term feeling of relief. However, it does not eliminate the feeling but simply relieves the pressure of it for the time being. Expressing is often unpleasant for the person toward whom we express our feelings and it sometimes causes further distress when we feel guilty for having done so.

3.   ESCAPE (Cope)
We turn on the TV, go to a movie, smoke, go out, play music, or have a drink, etc.--anything to get away from that unsettling feeling. But it doesn't go away--it's still there. It just goes underground, taking its toll on you even though you're not aware of it.

4.   RELEASE
This technique allows you to let go of the feeling itself. It is the healthiest and best way to handle a feeling. Each time you use the technique, you eliminate a bit of the repressed negative energy. It is a way of gradually discharging the suppressed energy of the feeling until eventually all the suppressed energy is undone, leaving you freer and calmer. As time goes by, you become naturally free and calm, with greater clarity of mind. Purpose and direction become more positive and constructive, resulting in better decision making and increased productivity.

Chapter 3

CHAPTER FOUR

THE METHOD OF RELEASING

"Happiness is calmness with no emotions or effort;
unhappiness involves energy, emotions and effort."
--Lester Levenson

I want you to think about somebody or some situation that is particularly agitating. (Try not to pick the worst thing in your life right now. We will build up to that. We learn how to crawl before we learn how to walk, so as you learn now to use the technique, you will eventually begin using it on more complex matters.) So think about some annoying person in your life, maybe in the office, maybe at home, or some situation that you would like to change. Point or tilt your head down slightly toward your stomach or chest area, which is your feeling center. This is the area where you can erase things. That's the erasing mode, the "erase" button. If you only access the head, all it does is it record and play back information. It does not erase thoughts or feelings. If you push the "erase" button and access your stomach or chest, you will be in the erasing mode.

Because this is such a new and different concept, let's play with it and try it so you can comprehend the experience. So think about a person or situation that is not so wonderful in your life. Point or tilt your head down toward your feeling center (your stomach or chest). This disengages your head and activates the feeling center, which is the erase mode. You will notice an unwanted energy in your stomach or chest area. Take some time to notice it. We are just looking for some energy out of harmony in that area. Maybe it is a clutching feeling or a knot in that area. Again, notice that it is an unwanted energy.

The way one drills for oil is to first find the oil and then sink a rig or pipe into the oil pocket. Next, the pipe is uncapped and then the oil or energy comes shooting out. In Kuwait, the oil rigs were capped with cement in order to stop the oil from bursting out after Saddam Hussein tried to destroy the oil fields. Now, this unwanted energy that is trapped in our stomach and our chest WANTS to leave. The problem is it will not leave if you access your head. It will only leave from your stomach or your chest. So, once again, think about that situation or person that is particularly bothersome. Put your head down. Put an imaginary tube into that unwanted energy, uncap it and allow it to come shooting out.

Now allow more to come shooting out. And more. And more and more...

Notice if you feel lighter. All we are looking for right now is a little sign of lightness to show you that you can erase things. You might already see that when you think about that undesirable situation or undesirable person, you are not as bothered as you were before--just a second ago. Now think again about some situation or person that is not so wonderful in your life, put an imaginary rig or tube into that energy, that unwanted energy, uncap the tube and allow that energy to come shooting out.

If there is more negative energy there, it means you have to go deeper. So put the tube into the energy, go deeper into that unwanted energy and allow it to come passing through. And more. And more, and even more.... Now think of something that agitates you, or that aggravates you. Notice there is an unwanted energy in your stomach or chest by putting your head down. This disengages your head and you will notice an unwanted clutching in your stomach or chest. And could you just allow that energy to leave? Invite it up out of the tube. And more. And more, and even more! If you find an unwanted energy in your stomach or chest and the rig and tube allusions are not working for you, can you instead create an imaginary window right where the energy is? Where this agitation is? Open up the window--wide open--and just allow the energy to leave through the window. And more. And more, and even more!

Take a check and see if you are as bothered as you were a second ago, before you let this energy go. Again, we are just looking for a lighter feeling. We are more or less crawling around right now, exploring how to use this wonderful technique. It is different, but everybody can do it. So let's just experiment with it some more.

See if you can bring up something else that agitates you--something that is aggravating or something that perturbs you. Can you allow that energy to come up? Invite it up from your stomach or your chest, and just allow it to pass through. And more, and even more. It is important not to judge this unwanted energy. Just say to yourself, "It's not good, it's not bad, it is just phenomena passing through." See if you can see it only as phenomena just passing through. And more, and more. You do not need to analyze it, you need only to allow it to pass through. Remember, you do not want to analyze a splinter, you only need to pull it out. And more. And more...

Now, think of something that frightens you--maybe something from the past. Point your head down--disengage it. Again, look for that unwanted feeling in your stomach or your chest area and just allow that energy to come passing through. It wants to leave if you disengage your head and activate the release mode, which is your stomach or chest area. Could you allow that energy to leave? And even more? Think of something else that bothers you or some situation that is not so wonderful in your life. Can you allow that energy to come up and just allow it to pass through? It's not good, it's not bad. It is just energy passing through.

Now what we would like to do is allow ANY energy to pass through. Good energy, bad energy--just see ALL ENERGY as phenomena passing through because, if it is good, we will try to hold on to it, thus STOPPING the releasing process. If it is bad, we will try to suppress it, again STOPPING the releasing process! We must be able to allow ALL energy to come passing through. Remember, all it wants is to leave, so just allow it to leave by opening up your release mode.

Now think of someone in your office or at home--somebody in your life that is annoying. Tilt your head down, disengage your recording unit. Notice you have an unwanted energy in your stomach or chest. Allow that energy to come up and allow it to pass through. Allow some more to pass through. Now take a check to see if you are as bothered as you were before you thought about the situation. Chances are you are not, proving to yourself that this sound in your head can be erased!

Many times there will be residual energy still lodged inside. You might have picked a difficult circumstance, a deep-seated, deep-rooted situation to examine. This only means you need to release on it some more. After all, it could have been there for quite a long time.

Being a physicist, Lester Levenson knew quite a lot about energy. He said this unwanted energy is smaller than a photon particle. Every time something aggravates us, what do we do with it? We suppress it, we stuff it, we shove it back down into our subconscious mind because it is too agitating to concentrate on. We do not want to listen to it, we do not want to see it, we want to get rid of it--so we stuff it! Each time some little aggravation occurs (e.g., someone steps on our toes, someone yells at us or disappoints us, someone cuts us off in traffic) what are we doing with this energy? We are stuffing it. This energy continues building up in us the older we get. When we store up enough of this energy--again, it is smaller than a photon particle and is actually measurable--it starts to fill our bodies and begins to press against our organs, our stomach lining, our back area. This is what causes headaches, body aches, and other unpleasant body sensations. When it builds up, it causes the body and the organs to stop functioning properly.

This energy can be dispelled and when we let this energy go, it allows the body to normalize and function properly. The body is the perfect doctor if it is not impaired with all this negative energy.

Contemplate some more energy you could let go. Just allow this energy to come up and just allow it to pass through, knowing that it is neither good, nor bad--just phenomena passing through. And more, and even more!

What else do we do with this energy? Some of us express it. We start screaming and yelling or crying. As soon as this negative energy builds up and becomes bothersome, what do we do with it? We go right back to stuffing it, then we start suppressing it or we try to escape it. We take a vacation, we listen to music, we take a drink. However, when we again become conscious--there it is. It continues to bother us, so we go right back to stuffing and suppressing it.

What we are examining right now is un-suppressing. We are learning to bring up the energy which can be erased, allowing it to come forth and pass through. Just like the Kuwait situation we mentioned earlier, the oil wells had to be capped with cement to stop the oil from escaping. Our energy is very similar--it wants to leave. Just keep the releasing mode open. Like a muscle, "The RELEASE® Technique" should be exercised. Once you start to practice it--and the more you practice it--you will find it becomes more pleasant and easier to do.

For example, if you plan to drive your car, it would be a bad idea to keep your eyes closed or your head pointed down. However, you could place your hand on your feeling center (your stomach, chest or wherever you feel this energy), just as a reminder to release from that area. This will prompt you to release from your feeling center instead of accessing your head, which cannot activate the erase mode for you. You can put your hand on your stomach or your chest wherever you feel this unwanted energy. That action will remind you where the energy is, to get out of your head and to let the energy go from your feeling center.

Again, let us think about another person or situation that is agitating (or perhaps the same one which is harboring residual energy). Could you just allow that energy to come up and just allow it to pass through? And more. And even more?

All of us have different ways of releasing this energy. Let us observe a fireplace and how it works. If we make a fire and do not open up the flue, what happens? The room fills with smoke and we start coughing. The same is true about letting our negative energy go. When we open up the flue, what happens to the smoke? It easily leaves. It takes no effort. All we need to do is open up the flue and the particles of smoke just float out. It is the same with feelings. This energy easily flows out. Can you allow some more energy to leave? Could you allow more? And even more to flow out?

Think of something else that has bothered you, that is not so wonderful in your life. Can you allow that energy to come up in your stomach or chest and then just allow it to pass through? Try more, and more...

Confusion is also just energy. Using this technique, one never has to be confused again. Try thinking about something that confuses you. Put your head down--disengage it. Put the magical tube into that unwanted energy and just allow the confusion to leave. Permit that confusing energy to surface and allow it to pass through. And allow some more, and even more. Now check to see if you feel clearer. Put your head down. You should be feeling lighter and lighter and clearer and clearer. This lets you know you are moving in the right direction. Continue to allow this confusion to come up and pass through. It is not good, it is not bad, it is just phenomena. And more, and more. And even more.... Now think of something else that confuses you. It is just energy. Can you see it only as energy? Just phenomena passing through? Disengage your head. Put your head down or put your hand on your feeling center and just allow this energy to pass through. And more, and even more. Notice that you are probably getting lighter. It is a pleasant feeling. So can you allow more of this energy to come up and pass through? Do not close the releasing muscle down; keep the tube open. This energy is not good, nor bad, it is just phenomena passing through.

So when you find yourself in any situation, you can always choose to put your magical tube into the energy, asking it to come up, inviting it up--it wants to leave--and just allow it to pass through. Know that you cannot release someone else's energy, but you can release your own. This will allow you to feel good all of the time, no matter what is happening.

Reflect on something else that bothers you in your life. Invite this energy up and just allow it to pass through. Allow more, and even more. Know that it is neither good nor bad, but merely phenomena passing through. And more, and even more.... Think about something else that agitates you. Just allow this energy to come up. It is in your stomach or chest and it wants to leave. Just allow it to pass through. And more, and even more.

Now, think about something in your life you would like to control--think of something you would like to be different. Put your head down and notice the feeling of wanting to change this thing. This wanting to control again invokes an unwanted energy, a lacking energy. Put the tube into that energy and just allow it to come up and pass through. It is not good, it is not bad, it is just energy passing through, leaving. And more, and more....

Now think of something else you want to change in your life--something you wish never happened. Put your head down and notice immediately an unwanted energy coming up. Just allow that energy to pass through. And more and more....

This technique also works on tiredness, hunger and numerous other feelings. Try using it the next time you are tired or hungry or do not want to surrender to a feeling. Merely disengage your head, put your head down or touch your feeling center, and allow that energy to come up and pass through. If you are tired right now, try closing this book, put your head down and notice that you have an unwanted energy in your stomach or chest. Allow that energy to pass through--it is not good, it is not bad and you don't have to figure it out! Just let it go!

Look to see if you are hungry or have thoughts about eating. Again, disengage your head. Notice you have an unwanted energy in your stomach or chest. Invite that energy up and allow it to pass through. If you are feeling a little light-headed, which is possible, allow the energy to continue to pass through. Do not try to stop it nor try to analyze it--just allow it to pass through. And more, and even more.

HOW WE SEE THE WORLD

Each and every one of us are naturally positive. However, we try to use our head to analyze things, and this blinds us to seeing what we really are. Similarly, if we had a beautiful table covered with dust, but we took a cloth and wiped, or we blew the dust off, what looked like an ugly table now shines forth--it becomes a beautiful table. The same is true about our feelings. Our feelings cover up or hide the beauty within us. So, if we disengage our heads, touch our feeling centers and allow unwanted or negative energy to come up and pass through, it just leaves. And what you will see and experience is this beautiful thing: YOU!

Let us pretend we are looking at the world through rose-colored glasses. All we see is the color of roses. However, when we take the glasses off, we have an entirely different picture. So it is with our feelings. If we just invite the feelings up, put the tube into the energy and allow it to pass through, the picture will begin to change. Take a check and see if this is not already so. Reflect on those things that bothered you before practicing this exercise. Notice that you probably feel these things just do not bother you anymore, or perhaps you are less bothered and now feel positive about them.

Now let's look at a goal you have been working on--something that you have not yet been able to accomplish in your life. Disengage your head down. You will notice an unwanted energy immediately shows up in your stomach or your chest. Allow this energy to come up and just allow it to pass through. And more, and even more. Now take a check and see if it is more possible to accomplish the goal or less possible--just with a little releasing. Every time you can let go of this energy, you take a step closer to "I can" and move farther away from "I can't."

Remember we are just crawling around on the ground and exploring what it feels like to release, to let go.

Up to now, what we have engaged in is suppressing, expressing or escaping our feelings. What we are doing now is releasing, letting go. So we need to spend time playing around with this concept. If it seems to a little difficult, do not worry about that. In time, you will discover this natural ability has always been with you. You might take a minute and explore around--be a cartoon microscope in a Disney movie. Look to see if there is any unwanted energy hanging around. Perhaps you feel you do not understand this releasing concept. Notice that will also bring up unwanted energy in your feeling center. Bravo! Put your magical tube into that energy or open up the window or the chimney flue. Just allow that energy to surface and pass through. Try some more, and even more, and even more! And as long as you are doing this, invite up some MORE unwanted energy.

Choose another bothersome something, anything which is not joyful in your life. Invite it up, IT WANTS TO LEAVE, and allow it to come up and pass through. It is not good, it is not bad, it is just phenomena passing through. More, and even more. Invite some more up. Invite some fear: anything that makes you frightened. Put your head down, see how this is an unwanted energy and just allow it to pass through. And more, and even more... Remember, we are merely looking for a light feeling--something that feels lighter.

This energy, which is smaller than a photon particle, is stored up in our body and actually can be weighed and measured. If we had a scientific device for measuring energy, we would actually see or measure this energy leaving us. The energy IS leaving and THAT is the LIGHT FEELING. So could you let go of some more? And more, and even more? Remember, this is just a beginning. You are learning to release. You can release with your eyes open or eyes closed. It is a good idea to practice using both techniques, eyes open, eyes closed.

As an assignment, play around with what you have just learned. As you move through a day, watch what happens. Look for the feeling in your stomach or chest. When you find an unwanted feeling, disengage your head or place your hand on your feeling center and allow the energy to come up and pass through.

CHAPTER FIVE

DUMPING NEGATIVITY AND LETTING GO OF RESISTANCE

When one learns, by actually experiencing it,
that the mind is only reactive, he then holds in mind
only the things he wants and never takes thought
for the things he doesn't want.
--Lester Levenson

In this chapter, we will be going even deeper into the releasing activity. In the preceding chapter, we looked at the negative energy in the form of feelings we have trapped in our stomachs and chests, finding that by acknowledging them and putting a magical conduit into this unwanted energy, we could allow it to surface and pass through easily.

Always see it as passing through--it is not good, it is not bad, it is just phenomena. By doing this continuously, you will begin to notice you are feeling much lighter about situations and people who previously used to bother you. If you have not experienced this yet, do not be concerned. Either return to the previous chapter and repeat the instructions or simply proceed ahead. It is all up to you! Remember, releasing is something that we all naturally use, but we use it unconsciously. With continual practice, we begin to use it consciously. Releasing is a method for rapid, on-the-spot change. It is quite easy and only takes seconds to do. You will soon find that you can defuse any problems in your life as they arise, simply by releasing.

Now let us look at resistance. What stops us from having all the good things in life? What stops us from releasing all the time?

Picture someone you have been resisting. Recall what you just don't like about that person. Now think again about that person and really feel the resistance within. Notice where it shows up. Does it feel like a clutching sensation in your stomach or chest?

Now ask yourself, "Could I let go of clutching? Just let it go, release it and allow that energy to pass through?" Could you let go of resisting some more? And more, and more.

Let me show you how to do some introspection about resisting someone. If you are resisting someone or something, you are experiencing a "push." Ask yourself, "Who is actually the pusher?" Perhaps if you were not resisting, you would not experience a push. That's something to ponder. The approach can be compared to the martial arts practices of aikido, karate, judo and/or tai chi. By using "The RELEASE® Technique", you will be able to defuse an opposing force without having to waste energy necessary to counter-control the pushing force. In other words, you can use the technique during an argument and find yourself in control simply by "letting go." Take a check: Test this yourself and see if it is not so!

In any event, just by feeling your resistance and letting go, that energy, too, will just pass through.

Now think of someone else you have been resisting. Notice you are clutching in your stomach or your chest. Tilt your head down and allow that unwanted energy to come up and pass through. And more, and more. Could you let go of clutching? Could you let go of resisting? Just allow that unwanted energy to pass through--it really wants to leave. It is not good, it is not bad, it is just phenomena passing through. And more, and even more. And even more.

To illustrate, let's take the case of Mark, a man in his thirties who worked his way up the corporate ladder of a telecommunications company. He found himself being passed by for promotions time and again, which angered and perplexed him. After taking the Release Course he realized he had been sabotaging himself in two ways. First, he was resentful of his boss and acted indignant and defiantly argumentative. He created a very unapproachable wall around himself and was increasingly more uncooperative and explosive. This in turn made him an unlikely candidate for promotion. Second, he discovered a program in his mind that came from a negative and demeaning father who had told him repeatedly he never would amount to anything. He saw how subconsciously he made sure to stay in a lowly position so his "supposed" incompetence would not be found out. Upon these realizations he released these programs and almost over night changed his situation. Soon after he was promoted to senior V.P.

In any conflict, it is important to look for the clutching, the resisting, because if one is resisting, one is experiencing a push from the other. We need to clearly see this: It is our resistance that causes us to experience a push from another person. So who is the pusher if you are NOT resisting? When you just let go of clutching and allow that energy to pass through, you will see that you will not experience a push.

Carl Jung, the noted psychologist, posed the question, "Is it the things going on around you that are causing you distress, or is it your reaction to them?"

CHAPTER SIX

THE KEYS TO EMPOWERMENT:
WANTING EQUALS LACKING

We should strive to attain a desireless state.
As long as we have desire, we lack.
Lack and want are the same thing.
Wanting traps us in a world of limitation.
Wanting is the greatest enemy of joy!
--Lester Levenson

During the year 527 B.C., in the Orient, Buddha enunciated the Four Noble Truths:

Life is suffering.
The cause of suffering is desire.
Ending desire ends suffering.
Desire is ended by following the Eight-fold Noble Path.

Twenty-five hundred years later, we still desire. Our society teaches us to desire, to want things, and to work to get things. So we may be happy. Capitalism is based on fostering desire for goods and getting love through having possession, money, knowledge or power. We are a culture of desire and fulfilling desire.

This is not surprising: we have not learned the lesson of love taught by Christ two millennium ago either. Both teachings reach the same point in the end: to become desireless, to not want anything external to ourselves, means we rest in ourselves, whole, joyous and happy. In this state, our true nature is constant love, unending love, giving love. When we reach this desireless state we feel like we have it all.

Lester Levenson attained his own enlightenment and mastered a desireless state.

We are very fortunate to be the recepients of a method he designed precisely with us in mind--products of the 20th and 21st centuries with our inquisitive, high-tech/low-patience personality type.

Chapter 6

According to Lester, the practical key to mastering desire is realizing that:
*The absence of desire is serenity.
*Desire is a bottomless pit that can never be filled up.
*Desire is the mother of all emotions, the disturber of all peace.
*Desire is the disturbance of one's natural inherent peace and joy.
*Desire keeps one involved in trying to satiate the desires, consequently detracting one from his constant natural inherent happiness. In short, desire is the enemy of happiness and the source of misery.
*Desire is the start of all agitation.
*Desire is an artificially created lack.
*Desire is the source of all trouble.
*Desire is a mind disquieter.
*Desire only leads to misery and death.
*If one will stop thinking of something, the desire for it will disappear and he will have it.

Let us look at the subject of DESIRE or WANTING.

Take a few minutes and make a list of the things you WANT in life. Then make a list of the things you HAVE in life. List as many things as you can think of for each category.

WANTING - Is lack or the sensation of "LACKING"

WANT = LACK

WANT = DESIRE

WANTING IS THE OPPOSITE OF HAVING

WANTING IS HOLDING YOU BACK FROM HAVING EVERYTHING IN LIFE.

QUESTION:

WHAT VALUE AT ALL HAVE YOU EVER RECEIVED FROM THIS "SENSATION OF LACKING OR WANTING"?
EVERYONE WANTS SOMETHING; IT ARISES FROM THE PAIN OF NOT HAVING.

... SO WHY NOT "LET IT GO" AND HAVE IT ALL?

EXERCISE

Make a list of things you want in life.   Make a list of things you have in life.

More money	Good home
a boat	Huge mortgages
house by the sea	Good business
no worries	great husband
better cars	lovely cats
better body	dog
Great health	ok health.

Wanting is the exact opposite of having. Can anyone stand up and sit down at the same time? Is it ever possible? You will notice that the things you want in life are the very things you do not have. Do you wonder why?

The old adage of "the rich get richer and the poor get poorer" can easily be explained. A rich person is holding in mind "I have money." He does not want it--his consciousness is "I have it." A poor person is forever wanting it, wanting it, wanting it--and, therefore, he is creating lack, lack, lack. So know that want equals lack. Want is a lacking feeling. It is not suggested that you let go of wanting so that you end up with nothing. It is merely pointed out that if we let go of wanting, we would have. This is a real dilemma for the mind.

So let us now take a look at one of the things that you have on your want list--things you do not have. Put your head down or put your hand on your feeling center and notice that it brings up a lacking feeling in your stomach or chest. This wanting brings up a lacking feeling. Now allow that lacking feeling to come up--it wants to leave--and allow it to pass through. And more, and even more. In Psalm 23, it says "The Lord is my shepherd; I shall not *want*. Thou preparest a table before me...my cup runneth over." Socrates said "Real happiness is havng no *wants*." And now consider that same item on your want list. Notice if it is now more possible or less possible to have it now that you have released some unwanted energy connected to that desire. Keep releasing the want until you feel like you can have or not have it and the suffering is gone from your stomach or chest area. Once we let go of the wanting, we begin to see that we have entered a realm of "havingness" and we begin to feel that it is easier to have the things we previously thought were unattainable.

DESIRE'S NATURE

First, to want something means we feel we don't have it. We feel empty, lonely, lacking or deprived, and we believe if we possessed that object or had that experience, we'd feel filled up and we would be happy. So behind all desiring and seeking is (1) a motivation to be happy and (2) a belief that happiness lies in desire's fulfillment.

On the contrary, desire IS the problem. Being in a state of desire is suffering, wanting, lacking, hurting and looking to a future time when we will have the want and be happy. Want is the opposite of having. In this course, we will teach you how to master the dynamics of desire and wanting (a lacking feeling). It is perfectly OK to have anything. The "having" is not the problem. The problem is "wanting, and lacking feelings" which causes pain and inhibits receiving. Check the list of wants you have made and see if there is pain there for not having it. Notice: it's everything you don't have.

So the solution to the problem of wants and desires is threefold: (1) We let go of the want in order to end the pain of desire, which allows (2) the receiving of what formerly was a want and allows us to hold in mind HAVING, which allows it to come to you. Lastly, (3) feeling already complete, we may decide to let go of attaining that which was so important just moments before because we already feel happy right now.

You can have it all! If you want anything at all, you can have it, providing you let go of wanting it.

Releasing feelings and desires leads to firsthand understanding of the true nature of thinking, emotions, wants and desires. All these occur only in our mind. Only our belief in their being real (and the importance of thinking, feelings, wants and desires) gives them any reality. Once we see that they are not real, but simply feelings, we begin to experience the ultimate state we all seek --that of happiness, with no sorrow, love, joy and havingness. When the mind, which creates everything, is quiet, we become happy, complete and joyous.

You are not who you think you are. You are not your feelings. All that you believe or perceive about wants is an illusion. Simply release and find out that what you think is simply a feeling.

The mind is like an oven. Does an oven care what it bakes? If you put a shoe in the oven and turn it on, it bakes the shoe. The same thing applies to the mind. It does not care what you put in, it simply creates what you hold in mind.

So now let's see how we can correct this misunderstanding and turn wants into having.

A DEFINITION OF WANTS

1. Although wants are not feelings, they definitely have a "feel" to them. Wanting Approval has a kind of "gimme" feeling to it--a kind of soft neediness.

Wanting Control, on the other hand, has a harder feeling. It is a little more push and assertive.

2. Remember that a want is a lack.

3. Remember that there is nothing wrong with giving or receiving approval or being in control. It is not the actual state that limits us, but the "wanting" it.

4. Releasing on the wants is more powerful and deeper than releasing on the emotions and feelings. When you let go of a want, you are letting go of a piece of everything on the chart.

5. All pain and misery comes from wanting approval and control--which is another way of saying "wanting love." All joy and bliss comes from giving approval and giving up wanting control--which is another way of saying "giving love."

6. Control is not BAD. It is the wanting (lacking) control that we need to release. It's okay to be in control all the time, just let go of the lacking feeling. Approval is not BAD. Have all the approval you want. What's off is the wanting (lacking) approval. Just let go of the wanting (lacking) approval and you will have it. Being safe and secure is what you want. It is the wanting (lacking) to be safe and the wanting (lacking) to be secure that is off.

Let us examine "wants" a little more. Take a look at that thing you want so badly. Notice you have an unwanted energy in your stomach and chest: a lacking feeling. Could you just allow that lacking feeling to come up and allow it to pass through? And more, and even more? Now, take a check and see if you feel a little lighter about that wanting. If not, put your magical tube deeper into that energy and see if that unwanted energy is still there. Remember, want equals lack. It is actually a lacking feeling that you are holding on to. Could you allow that lacking feeling to leave? It wants to leave. It will leave from your stomach or your chest area. Just allow that feeling to come up and allow it to pass through. Now continue releasing on the other items in your list of "wants." As you concentrate on each of these wants or desires, tilt your head down, note if you are clutching or resisting and invite the unwanted energy to come up and allow it to pass through. Work on these items, one by one.

"Happiness is our basic nature. We becloud that basic nature with thoughts. Thoughts of lack, thoughts of want. When we want something, our mind becomes active in trying to acquire that and we are unhappy because we lack something that we say we must have. So we create unhappiness through desire. All unhappiness starts with desire. All trouble in the universe starts with desire. Because basically we are perfect, full, complete, whole. We need nothing until we artificially create need and then become unhappy thinking how can we fulfill that need. But now after that artificial unhappiness is set into motion, we call happiness undoing the unhappiness. That's what people consider happiness today. Happiness is undoing the artificially created unhappiness. So we satisfy these thoughts of desire and momentarily we still the thinking. And when we still the thinking, our natural infinite self is there all the time and feeling that, we call that happiness. Happiness is nothing but feeling your real, ultimate self, that is all it is! By releasing the desires you undo the thoughts--you drop back to the unlimited you. That's called happiness."

Lester Levenson

Take some time eliminating your wants and fall into happiness.

CHAPTER SEVEN

THE VICIOUS CIRCLE AND
THE UNSTUCK ROAD MAP

The Unstuck Chart Road Map

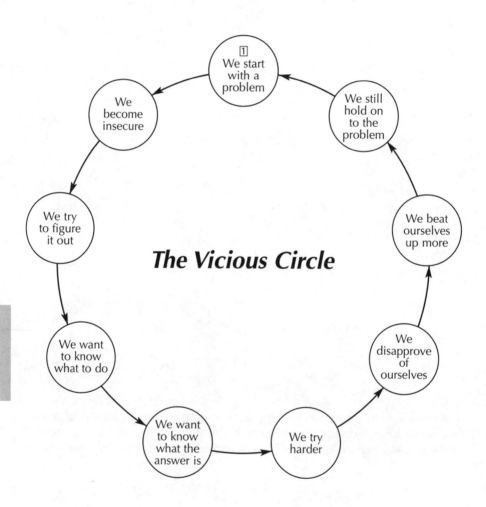

If we don't like what is happening to us in the world, all we have to do is change our consciousness--and the world out there changes for us! Once you realize that the road is the goal and that you are always on the road. Not to reach a goal, but to enjoy its beauty and its wisdom.

--Lester Levenson

Now let's look at another misunderstood subject: the habit of figuring things out. Refer to the previous chart as we continue examining this issue.

We start with a problem. The problem creates a feeling of insecurity within us. This feeling of insecurity triggers a desire to fix the problem, so we try and figure out how to solve it. But it persists, so we try harder to figure out how to solve it. To make matters worse, we then start to beat ourselves up for not solving it. We give ourselves disapproval and more disapproval. Meanwhile, the problem is still there and we fall back into the cycle again and again and it escalates.

Think about something you have been working on for a long time--a project, a goal, a health situation--something you have not been able to resolve. Here is what's probably going on:
You first have a problem
You then become insecure
You try to figure it out (by asking your mind for the answer and it doesn't have it)
You want to know what to do about it
You want to know what the answers are
Then you try harder
Then you start beating yourself up and you start disapproving of yourself
You still have the problem and you are right back where you started.

It is a continuous spin that can go on for years sometimes and cause more and more frustration.

So, now we will learn how to stop this spin or chain of events. Take a look at some illness that you had, some body ailment, or a goal about making money. Notice you have been trying to figure out what to do about it. You have not been able to get the answer. You are spinning around and spinning around and, because you do not get the answer, you start beating yourself up about it. Then you disapprove of yourself more and you still do not have an answer. Imagine kicking your car when it doesn't start or asking your computer for an answer. If the computer said, "I don't have an answer," would you beat it up? The smart thing to do is to find an automobile mechanic or another disk or program for your computer. Maybe then you would have an answer.

Imagine this: We keep asking our mind for the answer. Our mind says, "I don't have the answer." Then we beat it up. Why not listen to it? IT DOES NOT HAVE AN ANSWER. It is not suggested that you NOT get an answer--it is suggested that you need to LOOK TO ANOTHER PLACE for an answer. There is such a place, a higher place, that an answer can come from. This place is called beingness of true self or higher self. But one must be willing to leave the mind in order to find that place. Also, WANTING to figure it out is LACKING an answer--the mere WANTING is actually instructing the mind to NOT give an answer. It is a lacking instruction to the mind. So, again, we take a look at the situation or problem you have attempted to solve--whether it is a lack of money or perhaps an illness you wish to cure. Perhaps you consulted many doctors, read all kinds of self-help books, taken pills or other medications, but you still found no resolution to the condition. Perhaps it is a weight problem, or maybe you lack clarity in your life. The process of "WANTING" to figure things out goes on and on. Can you see where you have been wanting to figure it out?

Remember: WANT EQUALS LACK. So, ask yourself: COULD YOU LET GO of wanting to figure it out? JUST COULD YOU? AND WOULD YOU? AND WHEN? Without giving more thought to the WANT, just let it go! Letting go is like holding a pen in your hand. The tighter you hold on, the more it feels like part of you. Pick up a pen and hold it very tight. Next, open your hand and let the pen roll around loosely. Is the pen part of your hand or is your hand just holding on to it tightly? Now completely open your hand and let the pen fall. Notice how easily the pen drops from your hand and how nice that feels. The point of this exercise is to FEEL the pen drop away from your hand when you let it go. When we mistakenly hold on to WANTING feelings, we think that we are FEELING the anger, the grief or the fear. But if we let these go, we discover they are NOT US, but just FEELINGS--feelings that can be let go--just like when you let go of the pen from your hand a moment ago.

Look at your "want" situation. Can you see it brings up a clutching, a lacking feeling in your stomach or chest area? Can you put your head down and allow that energy to come up and just allow it to pass through--let go of that wanting, that lacking feeling? Could you let go of that lacking feeling? And more. And even more. And have you been wanting to know what to do about it? Could you let go of wanting to know what to do about it, that lacking feeling? Could you let go of wanting to know what the answers are? You might as well--your mind tells you that you don't know anyway. And more. And more. And even more. Now check and see if you feel a little lighter. Is it more possible to resolve the problem or less possible? Take a check. Put your head down and notice if there is anymore unwanted energy in your stomach or your chest --that LACKING energy. Could you let go of that lacking feeling, that clutching? Could you let go of clutching? And more. And more.

It is frustrating enough that we don't have an answer, but it is far more negative that we start beating ourselves up about it. It is like the earlier example of asking your computer for an answer and when the computer says, "I don't know what the answer is," we punch it and we beat it up. That is not going to get you an answer, but it is an old habit we all have. So take a look at the attitude or the habit of beating yourself up. Ask that energy to come up. Put your head down and just allow that energy to come up--that beating yourself up energy, that disapproving of yourself energy. Could you allow it to come up? Could you allow it to pass through? And more. And more. Put your head down and disconnect your mind and just allow that energy to come up and pass through. And more, and more. And more. See if you feel lighter. There is just a heaviness about beating yourself up. Could you ask some more beating-yourself-up energy to come up? Just allow it to come up and allow it to pass through. And more. And even more.

Could you give yourself some approval, just because--for no reason--just for the heck of it? And could you give yourself some more approval? And more? Could you just like yourself a little bit? Not much--just a little bit? And more. And more. And could you give yourself some more approval--just for the heck of it? And more. And more. And more.

Let us look again at the problem you have been working on. Is it more possible or less possible to overcome the problem or hurdle? Imagine dust covering up a beautiful table. It looks ugly because it is covered with dust. We cannot see how beautiful it is until we remove the dust. It is the same with our true self. Our negative feelings are covering up our inner perfection and beauty. Every time you let go, you get lighter and lighter. Every time you let go, you get closer and closer to what you really are--your true self--a positive limitless being. Take a check and see.

Take a look at the problem one more time. See if you have been trying to figure out what to do about it. Could you let go of WANTING to figure out what to do about it? Could you let go of WANTING to know what the answers are? You'd might as well--you don't know anyway. And could you let go of WANTING to know what to do about it? And more. And more. And even more. You are actually holding in mind the problem or holding on to wanting to figure it out. Your wanting is instructing the mind to give you a lacking energy. Notice that you are holding it in your stomach or your chest. Put your head down and allow that lacking energy to come up--that wanting--and allow it to pass through. And more. And more.

Now see if you have been disapproving of yourself or beating yourself up about the problem because you do not seem to have an answer. Just allow that energy to come up, that habit of disapproving yourself. We all have it. Just allow that energy to come up and pass through. It actually wants to leave. Disengage your head. Put your head down toward your stomach or your chest and invite this energy up and allow it to come up--welcome it up--and allow it to just pass through. And more. And even more. Could you give yourself some approval, just for the heck of it? No reason. And more. And more. Could you like yourself a little bit? Not much, just a little bit? Could you give yourself some more approval? Notice where it comes from: It comes from you. Could you give yourself some more approval? And more. And more.

Now take a look at the situation you have been working on. Is it more possible or less possible to overcome the problem? Take a check. Is it more possible to obtain or less possible? If you released, you fill find it is more possible.

The following exercise can be very helpful. It contains the releasing questions you should ask yourself, which we have been reviewing. Just ask yourself those questions: Could you let it go? Would you let it go? When? And more. Very simple.

YOUR TICKET TO BLISS AND ABUNDANCE
1. Could I let go of wanting to figure things out?
2. Could I let go of wanting to know what to do?
3. Could I let go of wanting to know the answers?
4. Could I let go of wanting to know anything (for this moment) right now?
5. And again. And again.
6. Could I let go of wanting to think?
7. And again. And again.
1. Now, can I let go of disapproving of myself right now?
2. And again. And again.
3. Could I give myself approval (for no reason)?
4. And again. And once more.

I have a fun assignment for you: I would like you to spend the next few hours looking for your wanting to figure it out. Look for it in your office, your home, your car--and every time you notice you are wanting to figure it out, stop immediately and let go of that wanting. Just let it go. It's just a habit. And every time you are disapproving of yourself, just put your head down, let the disapproving energy come up and allow it to pass through. Make sure to practice giving yourself approval. Look for it. It takes vigilance--it is just a habit in each of us. If you reverse this habit of wanting to figure it out (which is instructing your mind NOT to give you answers) and beating yourself up, you will begin to move closer and closer to having total abundance of health, wealth and happiness.

CHAPTER EIGHT

EMOTIONS--HOW TO MASTER THEM

If we really want to know the truth about who we are, all we have to do is let go of our attachment to thoughts and feelings. In silence, who and what we are makes itself known.
--Lester Levenson

In this chapter, we will review all we have been doing and then we will move further and take a step deeper into HOW to eliminate the habit of holding on to negative feelings--WHY it happened and WHAT to do about it.

We've been looking at our unwanted emotions by putting our head down. Every time we have an unwanted emotion, we put our head down or put our hand on our feeling center, stomach or chest, disconnecting our head and allowing the feelings to come up and pass through. Then we've looked at the wanting-to-figure-it-out habit. Actually, wanting to figure it out clouds your mind and allows you to be confused. It actually instructs your mind NOT to give you an answer. It's such a habit that it takes vigilance to reverse it, which is why I've asked you to spend the next few hours looking for the habit of wanting to figure it out and then let go of wanting to figure it out. Don't let it get further than your nose. And looking for the disapproval habit--disapproving of ourselves. It's a habit we all have--and let go of wanting to disapprove of ourselves. And feel the energy and allow it to come up and allow it to pass through. And also reverse the habit of disapproving ourselves by giving ourselves approval--liking ourselves. If you will notice, the more you do it, the nicer it feels and you will notice where approval comes from. It comes from inside yourself, and yet everybody is busy looking for it outside themselves. So practice giving yourself approval.

Now we are going to move on further and take a look at our feelings on a deeper level. I am going to ask you to read the chart of emotions which follows. Please read the chart, starting with the list of emotions under each category: Apathy, Grief, Fear, Lust, Anger, Pride, Courageousness, Acceptance and, finally, Peace. I want you to just sit and watch the feelings go by and notice that energy will get stirred up in your stomach or your chest. If it does, just allow it to pass through. Notice the flow of energy as you follow the chart. Lester called this the "AGFLAP" CHART: APATHY, GRIEF, FEAR, LUST, ANGER and PRIDE. Then we are going to move up to "CAP": COURAGE, ACCEPTANCE and PEACE.

Watch your energy as you move up the chart. Remember, these are just words--and watch how they affect you, if they do.

41

Chart of Imperturbability

Wanting to be Safe, Secure To Survive

Wanting Approval	Wanting Control

Apathy	Grief	Fear	Lust
Bored	Abandoned	Anxious	Abandon
Can't Win	Abused	Apprehensive	Anticipation
Careless	Accused	Cautious	Callous
Cold	Anguished	Clammy	Can't Wait
Cut-off	Ashamed	Cowardice	Compulsive
Dead	Betrayed	Defensive	Craving
Defeated	Blue	Distrust	Demanding
Depressed	Cheated	Doubt	Devious
Demoralized	Despair	Dread	Driven
Desolate	Disappointed	Embarrassed	Envy
Despair	Distraught	Evasive	Exploitative
Discouraged	Embarrassed	Foreboding	Fixated
Disillusioned	Forgotten	Frantic	Frenzy
Doomed	Guilty	Hesitant	Frustrated
Drained	Heartbroken	Horrified	Gluttonous
Failure	Heartache	Hysterical	Greedy
Forgetful	Heartsick	Inhibited	Hoarding
Futile	Helpless	Irrational	Hunger
Giving up	Hurt	Nausea	I want
Hardened	If only	Nervous	Impatient
Hopeless	Ignored	Panic	Lascivious
Humorless	Inadequate	Paralyzed	Lecherous
I can't	Inconsolable	Paranoid	Manipulative
I don't care	It's not fair	Scared	Miserly
I don't count	Left out	Secretive	Must have it
Inattentive	Longing	Shaky	Never enough
Indecisive	Loss	Shy	Never satisfied
Indifferent	Melancholy	Skeptical	Oblivious
Invisible	Misunderstood	Stage fright	Obsessed
It's too late	Mourning	Superstitious	Over-indulgent
Lazy	Neglected	Suspicious	Possessive
Let it wait	Nobody cares	Terse	Predatory
Listless	Nobody loves me	Terrified	Pushy
Loser	Nostalgia	Threatened	Reckless
Lost	Passed over	Timid	Ruthless
Negative	Pity	Trapped	Scheming
Numb	Poor me	Uncertain	Selfish
Overwhelmed	Regret	Uneasy	Voracious
Powerless	Rejected	Vulnerable	Wanton
Resigned	Remorse	Want to escape	
Shock	Sadness	Wary	
Spaced out	Sorrow	Worry	
Stoned	Tearful		
Stuck	Tormented		
Too tired	Tom		
Unfeeling	Tortured		
Unfocused	Unhappy		
Useless	Unloved		
Vague	Unwanted		
Waster	Vulnerable		
What's the use?	Why me?		
Why try?	Wounded		
Worthless			

Emotions

Wanting to be Safe, Secure
To Survive

| Wanting Approval | Wanting Control |

Anger	Pride	Courageousness	Acceptance	Peace
Abrasive	Above reproach	Adventurous	Abundance	Ageless
Aggressive	Aloof	Alert	Appreciative	Awareness
Annoyed	Arrogant	Alive	Balance	Being
Argumentative	Bigoted	Assured	Beautiful	Boundless
Belligerent	Boastful	Aware	Belonging	Calm
Boiling	Bored	Centered	Childlike	Centered
Brooding	Clever	Certain	Compassion	Complete
Caustic	Closed	Cheerful	Considerate	Eternal
Defiant	Complacent	Clairty	Delight	Free
Demanding	Conceited	Compassion	Elated	Fulfilled
Destructive	Contemptuous	Competent	Embracing	Glowing
Disgust	Cool	Confident	Empathy	Light
Explosive	Critical	Creative	Enriched	Oneness
Fierce	Disdain	Daring	Everything's ok	Perfection
Frustrated	Dogmatic	Decisive	Friendly	Pure
Fuming	False humility	Dynamic	Fullness	Quiet
Furious	False virtue	Eager	Gentle	Serenity
Harsh	Gloating	Enthusiastic	Glowing	Space
Hatred	Haughty	Exhilaration	Gracious	Still
Hostility	Holier than thou	Exploration	Harmonious	Timeless
Impatience	Hypocritical	Flexible	Harmony	Tranquility
Indignant	Icy	Focused	Intuitive	Unlimited
Irate	Isolated	Giving	In tune	Whole
Jealous	Judgmental	Happy	Joyful	
Livid	Know-it-all	Honorable]	Loving	
Mad	Narrow-minded	Humor	Magnanimous	
Mean	Never wrong	I can	Mellow	
Merciless	Opinionated	Independent	Naturalness	
Murderous	Overbearing	Initiative	Nothing to change	
Outraged	Patronizing	Integrity	Open	
Petulant	Pious	Invincible	Playful	
Pushy	Prejudiced	Loving	Radiant	
Rebellious	Presumptuous	Lucid	Receptive	
Resentment	Righteous	Motivated	Secure	
Resistant	Rigid	Non-resistant	Soft	
Revolted	Self-absorbed	Open	Tender	
Rude	Self-satisfied	Optimistic	Understanding	
Savage	Selfish	Perspective	Warm	
Simmering	Smug	Positive	Well-being	
Sizzling	Snobbish	Purposeful	Wonder	
Smoldering	Special	Receptive		
Spiteful	Spoiled	Resilient		
Steely	Stoic	Resourceful		
Stern	Stubborn	Responsive		
Stewing	Stuck-up	Secure		
Stubborn	Superior	Self-sufficient		
Sullen	Uncompromising	Sharp		
Vengeful	Unfeeling	Spontaneous		
Vicious	Unforgiving	Strong		
Violent	Unyielding	Supportive		
Volcanic	Vain	Tireless		
Wicked		Vigorous		
Willful		Visionary		
		Willing		
		Zest		

Energy Scale of Emotions

Emotion	Energy Used to Suppress	Energy Available for Action
The Negatives - AGFLAP		
Apathy	100%-95%	0-5%
Grief	94-90%	5-10%
Fear	89-85%	11-15%
Lust	84-80%	16-20%
Anger	79-70%	21-30%
Pride	69-60%	31-40%
The Positives - CAP		
Courageousness	59-35%	41-65%
Acceptance	34-15%	66-85%
Peace	14-0%	86-100%

The above scale illustrates how our natural, inherent energy is diverted into the task of suppressing, and keeping suppressed, the feelings (past decisions - past programs).

Our mind, the computer, in turn uses that energy to direct us into the thinking and patterns of behavior which have been predetermined by those past decisions or programs.

Now that you see how your mind works and how the emotions affect your energy, let's move on to the negative emotions, AGFLAP. Take them one by one, and you will see how each emotion affects your ability to discriminate; how it takes control over your "I" sense; and how you can help your "I" sense to start taking charge again. It is an exciting journey.

Now that you have read the entire chart, you probably noticed a shift in energy as you were reading. If there is any word category that resonated with you, look at that section again on the previous chart of emotions. Put your head down and see if it stirred up a want--an unwanted energy, a resistance, a clutching. Now just allow that energy to come up and allow it to move through. And more, and more. You might want to peruse this chart again and pay attention to your feelings as you read each category--AGFLAP: apathy, grief, fear, lust, anger, pride--and then move to CAP. Remember, keep releasing as you work through the chart.

Leaving AGFLAP Behind and Moving Up To Courageousness, Acceptance and Peace

We are now going to move up to CAP energy: C-A-P = courageousness, acceptance and peace--and these trump AGFLAP every time. We will move up to the real awareness of high energy and allow this energy to knock out the lower energy, to eat it up and dissolve it. You may want to take a few minutes first to review the AGFLAP chart and see if an unwanted energy is stirred up or is still there when you read the words. Just notice the energy in your body and allow the energy to come up and allow it to pass through. So take some time now before moving on. You might have noticed that the first word under the acceptance category is "abundance!" I am going to show you how to move up into this energy and stay there and allow yourself to have an abundance of everything in life.

STICKS AND STONES

Now see if you feel lighter, having let go of this energy. It is amazing how words can affect us. Notice the energy behind these words. Little kids have an expression: "Sticks and stones may break my bones, but names will never harm me." It is a nursery rhyme--and a good expression--but no one ever taught us how to accomplish this! For the first time, we are learning how to get to a place where nothing and nobody bothers us--a place of "imperturbability." Lester called imperturbability "the perfect place to be." Let us decide to make that our top goal for this course, OK?

MAKE IMPERTURBABILITY YOUR GOAL

If you look at the chart of emotions on pages 42-43, you will notice a word at the top of the chart: "imperturbability." That is the place where nothing and no one can ever bother us. Again, it's a place where you feel like you can have it all--a place where there are no impossibilities.

The previous pages provide a more comprehensive description of apathy, grief, fear, lust, anger, pride, courageousness, acceptance and peace, as well as help you to better understand these emotions and how to deal with them when they show up in life. Remember, keep releasing as you review these nine charts.

Read the following chart. Start at the bottom of the Scale of Actions, beginning with Apathy. Then move up the chart from the bottom to the top and notice the energy flow. Remember to keep releasing.

Scale of Action

Peace	I am - I am whole, complete, total unto my Self. Everyone and everything is part of my Self. It is all perfect.
Acceptance	No need to change anything. No judgments of good or bad. It just is and it's OK. It is beautiful as it is. I have and enjoy everything as it is.
Courageousness	The willingness to move out without fear or hesitation - to do - to correct - to change wherever needed. The willingness to let go - to move on.
Pride	The wish to maintain the status quo. Unwilling to change or move - therefore, the wish to stop others from movement as they might pass us up.
Anger	The desire to strike out to hurt and stop the other one, but with hesitation. We might or might not strike out.
Lust	The desire for possession - Wanting. The hunger for money - things - people, but with hesitation. We may or may not reach out. There is an underlying sense that we cannot, should not have.
Fear	The desire to strike out but not doing it because we think they will hit us harder. The desire to reach out but not doing it because we think we'll get hurt.
Grief	The desire for someone to help us because we can't do anything but we think maybe someone else can - we cry for that someone to do it.
Apathy	Desire is dead because it's no use. We can't do anything and no one else can help. We withdraw and play weak so as not to get hurt.

You will notice there is a line above "Pride" and anything from "Pride" down on the AGFLAP chart is an "I WON'T," "I CAN'T" feeling. Pride is a very strong energy and we will be examining it further as we get into this course because pride stops us from having abundance. It is a big, strong, negative energy. It sounds like "I won't," but underneath it is really a strong "I can't," which is covered up with "I won't." Can you do it? No, I don't want to do it. Can you do it? I don't wanna do it. Pride is a hiding place, and most people stuck in it do not know that the pride energy is really what stops one from moving up into courageousness, acceptance and peace. Now read, COURAGEOUSNESS again. This is the first move upward to "I CAN." People who hang out in courageousness are the doers of the world. Now read ACCEPTANCE. Then read PEACE.

Take a few minutes and just take a look at the scale of action chart and place yourself on the chart--see where your home base is. It is important to do this because using this chart will show you that you can move up the chart just by letting go. The more you prove this to yourself, the more you will use this to motivate yourself to release more. Every time you let go, you find yourself moving up and up. Ask yourself: Is your home base in apathy, grief, fear, lust, anger or pride? Or is it in courageousness, acceptance and peace? Do not judge yourself--don't make yourself wrong. It's not good, it's not bad. You just need to find out where you are so you know that you are moving upward as you begin to release. If we know that we are moving, we are encouraged to use this technique more and more. Every time you let go, you will discover that you move up. Each time you let go, you will feel lighter and lighter and happier and happier.

Notice there is a gray pyramid shape on the Scale of Action. The shading grows lighter toward the top. This illustrates how these emotions, suppressed over the years, are stacked in tighter and tighter as you reach the bottom of the chart. There are layers of feelings suppressed and covered up--one on top of the other. Every time we stuffed an anger, every time we stuffed a feeling of grief, every time we stuffed some AGFLAP, the energy got suppressed and is now stuck in our memory banks. As we start un-suppressing by releasing, this energy starts coming up because it is not supposed to be there and it wants to expend itself. It is important to be vigilant and allow this energy to come up and out. Don't judge it. It's not good, it's not bad--it's just coming up so it can leave. Remember every feeling wants to leave and we are actually holding them in. This is very important. Be vigilant of it. It is akin to a Kleenex box. When you take one tissue out, the next tissue comes up automatically. You take another one out and the next tissue comes up. And if you keep emptying out the box, eventually the box will be empty. It is the same with these suppressed emotions. Keep letting them go and eventually you will empty yourself of these disturbing emotions, and you will be home in a place called "imperturbability," where there are no more feelings that bother you anymore. As you release, one feeling will come up and the next feelings will come up. It might be joy, it might be followed by grief, it might be followed by anger. Just let them come up and allow them to pass through. If you get into the habit of not judging your feelings and see all feelings as simply phenomenon, you will discover they will just pass through with ease. Remember: feelings are not good, they are not bad--they are just passing through.

So let us do a little cleanup before we move on. Close your eyes or put your hand on your feeling center, your stomach or chest, and notice if you have an unwanted energy stirred up about what we just discussed. Could you allow that unwanted to come up and allow it to pass through? It's in your stomach or your chest. Disengage your head and allow that energy to come up and pass through. It's not good, it's not bad, it's just passing through. And more. And even more. Now see if there's some more unwanted energy that's stirred up. Could you allow it to come up and allow it to pass through? And more. And even more.

Now see if you are trying to figure something out. Could you let go of wanting to figure it out? And more. And more. And even more. And could you let go of wanting to know what to do about it? And more. And even more. And could you let go of wanting to know what the answers are? You'd might as well. You don't have the answer right now, anyway. And more. And more. You'd might as well let go and have answers by letting go of lacking. And more. And more. And notice if you've been disapproving of yourself. Could you allow that energy to come up and allow it to pass through? It's not good, it's not bad, it's just passing through. And more. And more. And even more. And could you give yourself some approval? Just for the heck of it? No reason necessary. And could you give yourself some more approval? And more. And even more. And even more. Notice how you feel right now. Notice if you feel more positive or less positive. You must prove to yourself that the more you release the more you prove to yourself that every time you let go you will get lighter and lighter and clearer and clearer. You will begin to move into courageousness and be able to move on; confront some of these other feelings that are long-term habits which seem to be difficult to let go. However, if you let go of clutching and let go of resisting, you will discover they are JUST FEELINGS. These feelings have been stopping us from having everything we want. And they are just feelings! Just play around with that and you will discover that's all it is. It's just energy and just allow it to pass through. It's not good, it's not bad, it's just phenomena passing through.

So, as we move on, we will be getting rid of wants (lacking feelings) and desires that actually have been subconsciously stopping us from having abundance.

The Emotional Picture
(How the Feeling of Desire Works)

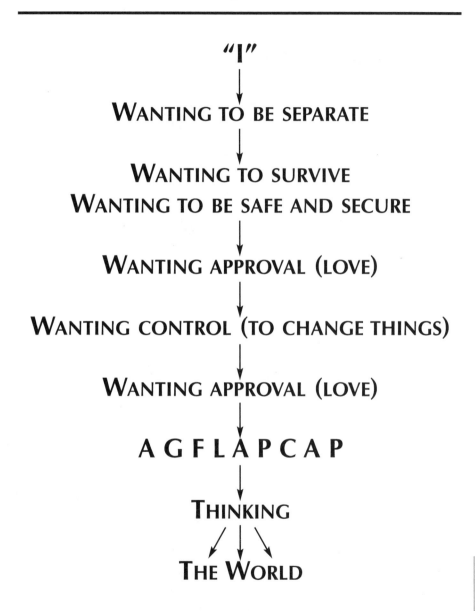

"I"
↓
WANTING TO BE SEPARATE
↓
WANTING TO SURVIVE
WANTING TO BE SAFE AND SECURE
↓
WANTING APPROVAL (LOVE)
↓
WANTING CONTROL (TO CHANGE THINGS)
↓
WANTING APPROVAL (LOVE)
↓
A G F L A P C A P
↓
THINKING
↙ ↓ ↘
THE WORLD

Chapter 8

CHAPTER NINE

THE ROOT CAUSE OF FEELINGS

We are unlimited beings limited only by the concepts of limitation we hold in our mind. So stop being what you are not, a limited body and mind, and just be what you are--an infinite, totally free, grand and flowing being, whole and complete.
--Lester Levenson

Let us examine the root cause of all feelings. How did the sensation of feelings get started and why are they running us and making us reactive? Here is how it begins: some incident occurs in our life. It stirs up our wanting to be safe, a "lacking safety" feeling, and we become insecure. Something somebody says or does makes us insecure and it stirs up our wanting to be safe, wanting to be secure and our wanting to survive. What happens when we feel insecure is we try to control the other person which stirs up our wanting to control. We have an out of control feeling. Therefore, we try to control the other person. If that does not work, we go to wanting approval, wanting to be loved. We try to be nice so people will not harm us, disturb us, or make us feel insecure. When we get insecure, we start to AGFLAP the other person--we pull out the tools of AGFLAP. We use apathy, grief, fear, lust, anger and pride against them.

As we hold on to all of our apathy, grief, fear, lust, anger and pride, these feelings actually cloud our picture of the world. It affects our thinking and clarity, causing us to see everything from a negative point of view. You have seen people who are angry--everything that happens in their lives is coming from an angry point of view. You have seen people who are in grief--everything that is happening to them is from a victim, "poor me," "boo hoo hoo" point of view. That affects the picture of your world because you are what you think you are. Let go of this picture and your world will change.

So we are going to practice letting go of wanting (lacking) approval, wanting control and wanting to be safe and secure.

What are some of the ways we try to seek approval? We try to be nice, we smile, we try to seem smart, we get a big job, a new car, a new suit, we dress sexily, act helpless--the list goes on. Think of some ways you try seeking approval. You might want to write them down on the following chart and examine them.

WAYS IN WHICH I SEEK APPROVAL (LOVE)

_____

_____

_____

_____

_____

_____

_____

_____

_____

Now what are some of the ways we seek control? We scream and yell, we put our nose up in the air. We don't talk to people, we walk to the other side of the street, we embarrass them, we ignore them, we make them feel guilty, we hire a lawyer, we call the police and so on. Think of ways that you try to seek control. You might want to write them down on the following chart and examine them.

WAYS IN WHICH I SEEK CONTROL (CHANGE)

_____

_____

_____

_____

_____

_____

_____

_____

_____

_____

_____

Now let's take a look at the ways you seek security, safety and survival. What do you do? You listen to your fears so you can be safe. You dare not fly high; you keep yourself down. You procrastinate and avoid making decisions. You act smart, you get to be powerful, you accumulate a lot of money, you buy a big house, and so on. So look at some of the ways you seek security, safety and survival. You have obsessive behavior like a myriad of doctor visits, taking numerous vitamins and other pills just to be safe. These are some of the things that stir your wanting to be safe (lacking safety).

Think of some of the ways you try to seek security, safety and survival. You might want to write them down on the following chart and examine them.

WAYS IN WHICH I SEEK SECURITY/SAFETY/SURVIVAL:

_____

_____

_____

_____

_____

_____

_____

_____

_____

In order to properly learn the Release Technique it is important that you see everything in life as a feeling of either WANTING APPROVAL, WANTING CONTROL or WANTING TO BE SAFE.

Think of something that bothers you in your life. Maybe it's a person. Does that stir up a feeling of wanting approval, control or safety? Whichever want that it stirs up, could you let go of either wanting approval, wanting control or wanting to be safe? Could you just let it go? Would you let it go if you could? And when would you let it go? Take a check and see how you feel about it now. Do not stop until you feel completely calm. Think of something that stirs up your wanting approval. Could you let go of wanting approval? Would you let go of wanting approval? When?

Take a check and see if you still want approval (and since "wanting" approval is a "lacking" feeling, you're lacking approval). Could you let that go? Would you let that go? And when?

Remember, these feelings are just feelings. Take a pencil or an object you have handy and clench it in your fist. Stretch your arm and hold on to the object real tight. And make your fist tighter--tighter--tighter--and even tighter. Now open up your hand and just let it go. Notice how easy it was. Notice there was no clutching after you let it go. Your hand just relaxed. And the more you held on to the object and the more you clutched, the tighter your hand got. This is exactly what we are doing with feelings. We are holding on to them. So when you let go of wanting approval, you are actually letting go of the lack feeling. Just let go of the lacking feeling the way you let go of the object in your hand. It's simple: You just let it go.

Now let us look at something you want to control--something you want to change. Could you let go of wanting to change it? Could you let go of wanting control--the lack of control? Would you let it go? Could you let it go? And when? Check and see if you feel lighter. And bring up some more wanting (lacking) control. Would you let it go if you could? When? See if this brings up a want-ing control in your stomach or chest area--a clutching, an unwanted energy. Could you just let go of wanting to control? Think of something you want to con-trol. Would you let it go if you could? Could you let it go? When? Just let it go. Just drop it. And more. And more. If you are having difficulty with it, you can put your head down. Feel the unwanted energy in your stomach or chest and just allow it to leave. Remember: Do not judge the feelings. They're not good, they're not bad, they're just passing through.

The Easy Way to Release
*Become aware of the feeling
*Feel the feeling
*Identify the feeling
*Relax into the feeling
*Release the feeling

Releasing Questions
Choose an incident from your past about which you still have some feel-ings.

Ask: What is your current feeling about the incident?

Does that bring up a Wanting (lacking) Approval? A Wanting (lacking) Control? or a Wanting (lacking) to be safe or secure?

Could you let it go?

Would you let it go?

When?

Now: Focus on the situation again and notice how you feel.

Is there more of that feeling left, or is there a different feeling?

Could you let it go?

Would you let it go?

When?

Continue the process:

Could you?--Would you?--When?

Continue the process until you are completely calm about the incident.

Think of something that stirs up the wanting to be safe and secure. A situation, a person. That lacking feeling it stirs up in you. Could you let go of that wanting to be safe and secure? Could you? Would you let it go? When? And now keep doing that until you feel calm about the situation.

The Easy Way To Release
Assignment: I would like you to spend the next few hours looking for the wanting approval, wanting control and wanting to be safe. See everything that's happening to you. Everything that people are doing as either wanting approval, wanting control or wanting to be safe. Look for it. Be vigilant! If you can't figure out whether it's wanting approval, wanting control or wanting to be safe, just let go of the contraction or unwanted energy in your stomach or chest, and allow it to leave. It's a wonderful way of looking at life and you'll notice that you will feel lighter and lighter and you will be moving closer and closer toward abundance and having everything you want in life. Please read the following chart called The Six Steps--this is the key to using The Release Technique to maximum degree!! I suggest you photocopy this sheet, you might want to reduce it and put it in your wallet or purse or tape it on your computer, or your mirror at home. It will remind you to release. Using this chart will take you all the way to imperturbability or freedom.

THE SIX STEPS

1. You must want imperturbability more than you want approval, control and security.

2. Decide you can do the Method and be imperturbable.

3. See all your feelings culminate in three wants—the want of approval, control and security/survival. See that immediately and immediately let go of the want of approval, want to control and the want of security/survival.

4. Make releasing constant.

5. If you are stuck, let go of wanting to control the stuckness.

6. Each time you release you are happier and lighter. If you release continually, you will be continually happier and lighter.

CHAPTER TEN

FINANCIAL ABUNDANCE
ATTACHMENTS and AVERSIONS TO MONEY

"When we know that we have everything and therefore need nothing, then everything comes to us for the mere effortless thought of it."
--Lester Levenson

According to Lester, the basic mechanism of desire is, first, we create a lack and then desire whatever is necessary to fill that lack. The desire creates thoughts. The thoughts cover the Self and this makes us unhappy. Then we look to relieve that unhappiness by fulfilling the desire which momentarily stills the thoughts. The stilling of thoughts removes a bit of the cover of the Self and it's feeling of a bit more of the Self that we call pleasure. We wrongly attribute that joy or pleasure to the thing or person that was used to fulfill the desire to relieve the agony of the thoughts of desire that were covering the Self. Because of this wrong attributing of the joy to the person or thing, the desire will never be satiated because the joy is not in the person or thing. The only possibility of satiety is to remain in your Self.

To go even deeper into releasing we will now introduce the element of ATTACHMENT and AVERSION. Attachments and aversions are two opposite forces which often run our lives. An *attachment* is a clinging desire to have and/or to hold on to something or someone. An *aversion* is a repulsion of, or an exreme desire to keep away from, something or someone.

Examples of attachments:
I'm attached to my mate.
I'd be lost if my lover left me--they give meaning to my life.
I'm attached to my station in life.
I like the respect that I get when people know how successful I am.
I'm attached to my title.
I love that people refer to me as Doctor (or substitute any title).
It gives me preferential treatment, everywhere I go.
I'm attached to my books.
I like being considered handsome.
I'd simply die if I became fat (lost my looks, my hair, looked old).

Examples of aversions:
I have an aversion to bad manners.
I hate rude people.
When people talk in a foul manner, I get very angry.

I have an aversion to 'cold call sales calls.'
It's really hard for me to fake being warm and friendly to people I don't
know.

Here again the desires keep things away from us subconsciously. Doing the Attachment and Aversion exercise brings up the subconscious feelings which show up in the form of "clutching" or "resistance". When we release these sub-conscious desires we can discriminate why we are doing destructive things to ourselves (subconsciously) and get rid of them easily. So we can be clear on what is holding us back, and get rid of what is holding us back in any area.

This exercise can be done on any subject, but for the first exercise we will start with ATTACHMENT AND AVERSION TO MONEY--THE WAY TO LET GO AND HAVE IT.

This is an important subject not only because it has such an important effect on our lives, but because just the subject itself stirs up our inner feelings, thoughts and attitudes about it. To the mind that is holding many limitations, negative thoughts, negative feelings and belief systems, money is a "problem." It is a source of endless worry and anxiety, hopelessness and despair or, ulti-mately, of vanity, pride, arrogance, intolerance of others, jealousy and envy. At its worst, the end result of all the negativity is poverty and a constant feeling of lack. Because of fear and limitations, the feeling of "I can't" is often avoided simply by avoiding the whole issue of money and accepting as inevitable a low socioeconomic status. The unconscious thoughts bring to us what we think we deserve. If our views of ourselves is small, limited and miserly (due to accumu-lated guilt), then the unconscious will bring those economic conditions into our lives. Our attitudes about money come up as we look at the many things that it means to different individuals (and to all of us, to some extent)--the degree to which it stands for security, power, glamour, sexual attraction, successful com-petition, self-worth, as well as our value to others in the world.

It is very useful to sit down with pencil and paper at this point. Under the heading "money," begin to delineate what its real meanings are in all the vari-ous avenues of life. Then begin to note the feelings that are associated with each area and begin to release on these negative feelings and attitudes. As we do this, we come up with our own answers about it.

Without being conscious of what money means to you emotionally, you are the effect of money. You are being run by money and all of its associated pro-grams. It is like the millionaire who keeps piling up more and more millions. There never seems to be enough. Why is that? It is because he has never stopped to look at and find out what money really means to him. The person who obses-sively chases money is doing so because his inner self-worth is so small that it takes a huge amount of money to compensate for it. The inner insecurity is so extensive that no amount of money can overcome it. It might be said that the smaller a person feels inside, the greater amount of power, money and glamour they must accumulate in order to try to compensate for it.

In the released state, money merely becomes a tool to achieve one's goals in the world because there is not that inner smallness, insecurity and low self-esteem. The person has the inner security of knowing there will always be sufficient abundance. They will always get what they need when they need it because there is an inner feeling of completion, fulfillment and satisfaction. In effect, money becomes a source of pleasure rather than a source of anxiety. A very released person has a different attitude about money. When they need it to complete a project, it just magically seems to appear from somewhere. They have no attachments or aversions to it because it no longer runs them. Because they are in a positive direction, money comes to them easily--without effort. Once you have the formula for gold, you do not need to carry a bag of it on your back with all of its attendant worries and anxieties. It is very common for graduates of The Release Technique to suddenly come into abundance.

Now we are going to look at our attachment to money. The first thing we do is let our minds run, just let a stream of consciousness flow. When you think about your attachment to money, see what is the first feeling or thought that comes up. Whatever it is, could you see that feeling or thought as wanting (lacking) approval, wanting (lacking) control or wanting (lacking) to be safe? Could you let go of either wanting approval, control or safety? It is just an unwanted energy that gets stirred up in your stomach or your chest area. Just let it pass through. And look at the subject again: attachment to money. See if it brings up a feeling--a wanting of approval, control or safety. Could you let go of wanting approval, wanting control or wanting to be safe? Remember we are not letting go of control, approval or safety, but only letting go of the lacking feelings. Now let's take a third look at your attachment to money. You want more, you haven't got enough, things like that. Whatever thoughts or feelings come up: perhaps "Other people have it, but I do not have enough", "Why do they have it and I do not?", or "No matter what I do, I cannot get it". See each feeling as either wanting approval, wanting control or wanting to be safe and let go of wanting approval, wanting control or wanting to be safe. Keep letting your mind flow until you completely run out of ideas about money to release on.

ATTACHMENT TO MONEY
Stream of Consciousness:
(Just let your mind think of things about the attachment. Write it down and see what you wrote or thought as wanting approval, wanting control, or wanting to be safe or secure and then release the want.)

What advantage is it to me to have money?

_____

_____

_____

_____

What disadvantage is it to me to have money?

_____

_____

_____

_____

1. Imagine never, ever being able to have money. (Let go of clutching or resisting the feeling it brings up in your stomach or chest. Keep releasing until there are no more feelings in your stomach or chest.)

2. Could I let go of my entire attachment to money? (Keep letting go until you can say yes 100% with no clutching or resistance.)

Now let us examine more of our subconscious mind. By probing deeper, we begin to see things clearer and we start to discriminate about what we are doing and why we are doing it. Then we stop doing it automatically and, finally, we can let it go. It is easy.

So, what advantage is it for you to have money? Write one down under the "Advantage" column. Does that bring up a feeling of wanting approval, control or safety? And whichever want it brings up, could you let go of either wanting approval, wanting control or wanting safety or security? And more. And more.

And what disadvantage is it for you to have money? Make something up--name something stupid, such as "People will bother me," "I'll have to pay a lot of taxes," or "People won't love me for my true self." Whatever thought or feeling that it brings up, can you see that as either wanting approval, wanting control or wanting to be safe and secure? And whichever want it is, could you just let go of either wanting approval, wanting control or wanting to be safe or secure?

Take a look at another advantage of having money that you might have. Whatever feeling it brings up, could you see that as wanting approval, wanting control or wanting safety and security? And whichever want it brings up, could you let go of either wanting approval, wanting control or wanting to be safe or secure? And now let's look at another disadvantage of having money. Give me one, make something up. Whatever it is, could you see that as wanting approval, wanting control or wanting to be safe and secure? And whichever want it is, could you just let it go? Look at another advantage of having money. Whichever want that brings up, could you see that as either wanting approval, wanting control or wanting to be safe or secure? Could you again let go of either wanting approval, wanting control or wanting to be safe and secure?

Next we will look at a disadvantage of having money. Make something up. Maybe you think you do not deserve it, maybe you are guilty, whatever. Could you see that as either wanting approval, wanting control or wanting to be safe? And could you let go of either wanting approval, wanting control or wanting to be safe or secure? And let's look at another advantage of having money. Does that bring up a feeling of wanting approval, wanting control or wanting to be safe or secure? And whichever want that brings up, could you let go of either wanting approval, wanting control or wanting to be safe and secure?

And now let us look at a disadvantage of having money. Whatever comes up, could you see it as a feeling of wanting approval, wanting control or wanting to be safe or secure? And whichever it is, could you just allow that feeling of wanting approval, control or safety and security to leave?

Sometimes we have the answer "none." If that comes up, you can ask yourself, is THAT wanting approval, wanting control or wanting to be safe or secure and then let THAT go? We often block our subconscious thoughts. Sometimes we even make ourselves numb in order to suppress the feelings and thoughts we do not want to acknowledge. We push them into our subconscious, but they are still in our minds and operating on a subliminal level. This may explain why you are not getting the abundance you think you deserve. Keep digging more into your subconscious mind, making you conscious of the feelings or thoughts you suppressed so you can now release them. This way they will stop operating and your situation will turn around.

The mind is like an oven. If you put a shoe into an oven and turn it on, the oven will bake the shoe. It really does not care what it bakes. The mind is like that oven: Put a thought in the mind and the mind will bake it, regardless of what it is. We put negative thoughts in our mind and they will stay there until we take them out--GARBAGE IN, GARBAGE OUT. If you are experiencing a numbing feeling, see THAT as wanting approval, wanting control or wanting to be safe or secure. Put your head down and let go of resisting that feeling. That, too, is just a feeling, so just allow it to pass through. We can unblock what is stopping, hiding in our subconscious thoughts. All we have to do is just make ourselves conscious of them and pull them out. That is what we are doing now. So one more: What advantage is it to have money?

Can you see that as wanting approval, wanting control or wanting to be safe? Whichever want this brings up, could you just let go of either wanting approval, control or safety and security? And one more disadvantage of having money? Whatever want that comes up, could you let go of wanting approval, control or safety and security?

GOING DEEPER INTO THE SUBCONSCIOUS MIND

Now, can you imagine never, ever, ever having money again? This brings up a lot of energy in our subconscious mind--and that energy is resistance. (Resistance effectively locks the energy of thoughts or programs in the mind-- the very ones we want out!) So I am asking what I call the "squeezing the lemon" questions. I will be asking them often to bring up this energy in our body so we can allow it to pass through. You will notice you will probably be clutching, resisting or just having a very uncomfortable feeling when you ask yourself that question. Just let that feeling come up and get rid of it. By ridding yourself of unwanted emotional feelings and thoughts, you will be moving closer and closer to opening your energy to allow the flow of abundance to come to you.

So, let us ask the question again and see if we have any more subconscious negative energy hidden away in our subconscious mind. Imagine never, ever, ever being able to have money again. Just put your head down and notice if there is an unwanted energy there. Let go of resisting and clutching and allow this energy to pass through. It wants to leave. It is not good, it is not bad, it is just energy--phenomena--passing through.

Again, let us ask the question: IMAGINE NEVER, EVER, EVER BEING ABLE TO HAVE MONEY AGAIN. YOU CANNOT HAVE IT IF YOU WANTED IT. Notice it brings up a lot of clutching, a lot of unwanted energy. Just allow that energy to come up and pass through. And more. And even more and more. Ask yourself the "squeezing the lemon" question one more time: IMAGINE NEVER, EVER, EVER BEING ABLE TO HAVE MONEY AGAIN. YOU CANNOT HAVE IT IF YOU WANTED IT. Notice it brings up a lot of unwanted energy, but it's getting lighter. And just allow that energy to pass through. And more. And more.

Ask yourself that question until you absolutely have no more feelings about that subject. Do this until the negative energy is completely gone. Then, as a check, ask yourself, "Could I let go of my entire attachment to money?" If that still brings up a clutching, a wanting, a desire, just let it come up, let go of holding on to it and allow the energy to pass through. It's just energy. It's not good, it's not bad, it's just a phenomenon passing through. Could you let go of your entire attachment to money? Could you allow it to come up and allow it to pass through? And more. And more. Continue releasing until you can say "yes" without any clutching, without any resistance. That is opening up the flow to further abundance and completely ridding yourself of this subconscious sabotage in the form of feelings and thoughts. Notice that you feel very light about the subject of money. That light feeling is the positive energy that you have been blocking in you with these negative feelings that you have been trying to avoid--you kept them because you did not have a better way out.

AVERSION TO MONEY--LET THAT GO AND STOP PUSHING MONEY AWAY

We will now begin to explore aversions to money. An aversion is a desire to get away. "Get that thing away from me." Why would we do something destructive to ourselves consciously? We would not, but it is your subconscious at work here. How do you know this is running? If you do not have enough money, you have a subconscious aversion to money.

AVERSION TO MONEY
Stream of Consciousness:
(Just let your mind think of things about the aversion. Write it down and see what you wrote or thought as wanting approval, wanting control, or wanting to be safe or secure and then release the want.)

What do I like about money?

_____

_____

_____

_____

What do I dislike about money?

_____

_____

_____

_____

1. Imagine always having money. (Let go of clutching or resisting the feeling it brings up in your stomach or chest. Keep releasing until there are no more feelings in your stomach or chest.)

2. Could I let go of my entire aversion to money? (Keep letting go until you can say yes 100% with no clutching or resistance.)

So when you think of the subject of an aversion to money, what feeling or thought does that bring up? Write those feelings under the stream of consciousness section on the diagram. And whichever feeling or thought that comes up, can you see that as wanting approval, wanting control or wanting to be safe or secure? And whichever want that it brings up, could you just let it pass through? And more. And more. If this leads you into wanting to figure it out, could you let go of wanting to figure it out? And more. And more. Look at your aversion to money again. Maybe what comes up is "I do not deserve it," "I'm not a good enough person" or "I do not have the right job". Whatever comes up, could you see that as either wanting approval, wanting control or wanting to be safe and secure? And could you let go of those wants? And more. And even more. Keep bringing up thoughts and feelings about the aversion to money until you have no more and then move on.

We will now ask some questions that are similar to advantages and disadvantages, but the mind is tricky. Therefore, we have discovered that by asking a question a little differently, it might bring up something different. If it brings up the same thing, that means you have not totally released on it. So then just release on it from that point of view.

So what do you like about money? Does that bring up a feeling of wanting approval, wanting control or wanting to be safe or secure? And whichever want that it brings up in you, could you let go of either wanting approval, wanting control or wanting to be safe or secure? And what do you dislike about money? Is that a feeling of wanting approval, wanting control or wanting safety and security? Remember that is also just an unwanted energy. Just allow it to come up and allow it to pass through.

What do you like about money? Does that bring up a feeling of wanting approval, control, or safety and security? And whichever want that it brings up, could you just allow it to leave? And more. And even more. And what do you dislike about money? Is that a feeling of wanting approval, wanting control or wanting safety or security? And whichever want that it brings up, could you just let go of either wanting approval, control, safety or security? And more. And even more. Keep going back and forth until you have no more likes or dislikes about money. Then move on.

Let's ask the "squeezing the lemon" question with regard to your aversion to money. Imagine always having money. You're loaded with it. See if that brings up a clutching, a resistance, an unwanted feeling in your stomach or your chest area and just allow it to come up and pass through. You might be surprised that you have a lot of resistance to having money; don't try to understand it. Just let go of that energy. And more. And even more. Again, let's ask the "squeezing the lemon" question. Imagine always having money. You're loaded with it. No matter what happens, you've got it. You can't get away from it. See if that brings up an unwanted energy, a strange feeling, resistance--a clutching feeling in your stomach or chest area. Could you allow that energy to come up? It's the subconscious thoughts and feelings that are stopping you from having abundance. Allow it to come up and just pass through. It's not good, it's not bad--it's just phenomenon. Remember that we don't have to figure out a splinter. If you notice it's there, what's the difference how it got there, what color it is, how big it is or who gave it to you? Just take a tweezer and pull it out. And that's what we're doing. Just allow that energy to leave, to pass through. Don't try to make sense out of subconscious negative thoughts and feelings.

Now let's "squeeze the lemon" again. Imagine always, always having money. You're loaded with it. You can't get away from it. And you know what to do: release any resistance or clutching energy.

CHAPTER ELEVEN

ATTACHMENTS AND AVERSIONS

The only thing that disturbs peace is desire.
--Lester Levenson

How to Do Attachments and Aversions on any Subject--Getting Rid of Your Subconscious Sabotaging Thoughts and Feelings

Maybe you have a habit, something you'd like to stop. Maybe there is a person that agitates you. Or a job situation that disturbs you. What follows are two sets of blank attachment and aversion sheets which you may want to make copies of for easy usage, keeping a blank set preserved for future occasions.

So pick a subject that you want to work on. We are going to analyze our attachment and aversions to this subject. And when you're ready, let's begin, by reviewing the chart on the next page.

Attachments & Aversions

Here again the desires keep things away from us subconsciously. Doing attachments and aversions brings up the subconscious feelings which show up in the form of "clutching" or resistance. When we release these subconscious desires, we can discriminate why we are doing destructive things to ourselves (subconsciously) and get rid of them easily, so we can be clear on what's holding us back and get rid of what's holding us back in any areas.

Attachments – A desire (wanting) to have it.	*Let go?
I am attached to my title at work – w/a *I like the respect it gets me when people know how important I am.* *I worked hard to get it and will continue to work to keep it.*	✓

INSTRUCTIONS:
1. Write attachment.
2. Write a stream-of-consciousness about attachment (just let your mind wander about the attachment).
3. Release on whatever wants are stirred up.
4. Do an *Advantage/Disadvantage* sheet.
5. Picture yourself never having this again, and release whatever comes up.
6. Ask yourself, "Could I let go of my attachment to _____?"
7. Then ask yourself the squeezing the lemon questions: Imagine never, ever having _____ again. Keep releasing until it is 100% okay.
8. Now ask yourself, "Can I let go of my entire attachment to _____?" Keep asking until there is no more clutching or resistance to saying yes.

Aversions – A desire (wanting) to get it away from me.	*Let go?
I have an aversion to cold-calling – w/s, w/a *I don't like calling people I don't know. I never know the* *right way to introduce myself.*	✓

INSTRUCTIONS:
1. Write Aversion.
2. Write a stream-of-consciousness about aversion.
3. Release on whatever wants are stirred up.
4. Do a *Likes/Dislikes* sheet.
5. Picture yourself never having this with you, and release what comes up.
6. Ask yourself, "Could I let go of my aversion to _____?"
7. Then ask yourself the squeezing the lemon questions: Imagine always having _____ ; you can't get away from it. Keep releasing until it is 100% okay.
8. Now ask yourself, "Can I let go of my entire aversion to _____?" Keep releasing until you can say yes 100%.

*Did I completely let go?

ATTACHMENT TO ...
Stream of Consciousness:
(Just let your mind think of things about the attachment. Write it down and see what you wrote or thought as wanting approval, wanting control, or wanting to be safe or secure and then release the want.)

What do I like about _____?

_____

_____

_____

_____

What do I dislike about _____?

_____

_____

_____

_____

1. Imagine always _____. (Put the attachment in the blank space and let go of clutching or resisting the feeling it brings up in your stomach or chest. Keep releasing until there are no more feelings in your stomach or chest.)

2. Could I let go of my entire attachment to _____? (Put the attachment in the blank space and keep letting go until you can say yes 100% with no clutching or resistance.)

On the sheet provided, write the subject you're working on next to "attachment to--" at the top of the page. Then do a stream of consciousness to that attachment. Keep releasing until you have no more feelings on that subject. Now let's move down the page to the "advantage" and "disadvantage" columns.

In the space provided, describe what the advantage is to you for being in or experiencing your situation. Hereafter, I'll just guide you by saying: "What advantage is it to you to have [blank]?" and you'll know to complete the phrase with your releasing topic.

Can you see what you wrote as wanting approval, wanting control or wanting to be safe? And whichever want it stirs up, could you let go of either wanting approval, wanting control or wanting to be safe? And what disadvantage is it to you to have _____? Does that bring up a wanting of approval, a wanting of control or a desire to be safe? Whichever want it stirs up, could you let go of either wanting approval, wanting control or wanting to be safe?

And what's another advantage to having _____? Does that bring up wanting approval, wanting control or wanting to be safe? And whichever want that brings up, could you let it go? And what's a disadvantage of having ____? Does that bring up a wanting of approval, a wanting of control or a wanting to be safe? And which ever want gets stirred up, could you let it go? And what's another advantage of having _____? Could you see that as wanting approval, wanting control or wanting to be safe? And could you let go of either wanting approval, wanting control or wanting to be safe?

And what's a disadvantage to you being/experiencing _____? Could you see that as a wanting approval, wanting control or wanting to be safe? And could you let go of either wanting approval, wanting control or wanting to be safe? And what's another advantage to _____? And could you see that as wanting approval, wanting control or wanting to be safe? And what's another disadvantage to _____? And could you see that as wanting approval, wanting control or wanting to be safe? And could you let it go?

And now let's ask the "squeezing the lemon" question: Imagine never, ever, ever being able to _____. Imagine never, ever, ever being able to _____. If that brings up a resistance, put your head down and allow that energy to come up and allow it to pass through. Imagine never, ever, ever being able to _____ and just allow that energy to come up and just allow it to pass through. It's not good, it's not bad--it's just phenomenon passing through. And one more time: Imagine never, ever, ever being able to _____. Does that bring up a wanting of approval, a wanting of control or a wanting to be safe? And which ever want it brings up, could you allow it to come up and could you let it go? Keep releasing until you have no more energy, clutching or resistance left in your stomach or chest areas. Now let's move on to the final question to see if there is any more energy left: Could you let go of your entire attachment to _____?

If there's any resistance or clutching to saying yes, allow that energy to come up, put your head down and allow that energy to come up and pass through. And more, and more.

Could you let go of your entire attachment to _____? Just allow that energy to pass through.

And now let's do an aversion to the exact subject you have previously released on in the attachment area. Remember, in order to rid yourself of the entire problem, you MUST release on BOTH sides in order for the problem, habit or situation to be entirely gone from your consciousness.

AVERSION TO ...
Stream of Consciousness:
(Just let your mind think of things about the aversion. Write it down and see what you wrote or thought as wanting approval, wanting control, or wanting to be safe or secure and then release the want.)

What do I like about _____?

_____

_____

_____

_____

What do I dislike about _____?

_____

_____

_____

_____

1. Imagine always _____. (Put the aversion in the blank space and let go of clutching or resisting the feeling it brings up in your stomach or chest. Keep releasing until there are no more feelings in your stomach or chest.)

2. Could I let go of my entire aversion to _____? (Put the aversion in the blank space and keep letting go until you can say yes 100% with no clutching or resistance.)

What do you like about _____? Does that bring up wanting approval, wanting control or wanting to be safe? And could you let go of either wanting approval, wanting control or wanting to be safe? And what don't you like about _____? Does that bring up a wanting of approval, a wanting of control or a wanting to be safe? And what do you like about _____? Does that bring up a wanting of approval, a wanting of control, or a wanting to be safe? And could you let go of whatever want that gets stirred up? And what don't you like about _____? Whichever want gets stirred up, could you let it go? And one more: What do you like about _____? Does that bring up a wanting of approval, a wanting of control or a wanting to be safe? And whichever want that has been stirred up, could you let it go? And what don't you like about _____? Could you let it go, whichever want gets stirred up?

Keep going back and forth and releasing until you have no more advantages or disadvantages on that subject you are working on. Now, let's ask the "squeeze the lemon" question regarding the EXACT subject--Imagine always having _____. Put your head down and see if that brings up an unwanted energy, a resistance. Just allow that energy to come up and allow it to pass through. Imagine always having _____. Put your head down. See if you're rejecting or resisting and allow that energy to come up and pass through. And could you let go of your entire aversion to _____? Just allow that to come up and allow it to pass through. Any resistance to saying yes? Put your head down, just let the energy come up and allow it to pass through. And one more: Could you let go of your entire aversion to _____? Any resistance to saying yes? Let it come up and just allow it to pass through. Keep releasing until you have no more resistance to saying, "Yes, I can let go of my entire aversion to _____."

Now I suggest you work on something on your own--a person, thing, situation, a smoking habit, eating habit, money issues--any kind of situation, any person that you can describe on the attachments and aversions pages. (Use the blank sheets in this book or make photocopies so you can have unlimited sets of attachments and aversions to use any time you want them. Many people simply write the chart on a plain piece of paper and release that way. It's a short chart and easy to do, too!) The more you perform this task, the more you will see how it helps you discriminate, to see things clearly and help you take yourself off "automatic."

See if that brings up any energy in your stomach or your chest area. Tilt your head down and allow that energy to pass through. Or put your hand on your stomach or your chest area and allow that to pass through. And more. And even more.

Imagine always having _____; you're loaded with it. You can't get away from it. Whichever energy that brings up, could you just allow it to pass through? And more? And even more? Just let go of resisting it. It's just an energy.

And now let's ask the final question: Can I let go of my entire aversion to _____ and release until I am 100% free.

ATTACHMENT TO ...
Stream of Consciousness::
(Just let your mind think of things about the attachment. Write it down and see what you wrote or thought as wanting approval, wanting control or wanting to be safe or secure and then release the want.)

What advantage is it to me to _____ ? What disadvantage is it to me to _____ ? (Always put the same attachment in the blank space.)

1. Imagine never, ever being able to _____ .
(Put the attachment in the blank space and let go of clutching or resisting the feeling it brings up in your stomach or chest. Keep releasing until there are no more feelings in your stomach or chest.)
2. Could I let go of my entire attachment to _____ ?
(Put the attachment in the blank space and keep letting go until you can say "yes" 100% with no clutching or resistance.

AVERSION TO ...
Stream of Consciousness:
(Just let your mind think of things about the aversion. Write it down and see what you wrote or thought as wanting approval, wanting control or wanting to be safe or secure and then release the want.)

What do I like about _____ ?
What do I dislike about _____ ?

(Always put the same aversion in the blank space.)
1. Imagine always _____ ?
(Put the aversion in the blank space and let go of clutching or resisting the feeling it brings up in your stomach or chest. Keep releasing until there are no more feelings in your stomach or chest.)
2. Could I let go of my entire aversion to _____ ?
(Put the aversion in the blank space and keep letting go until you can say "yes" 100% with no clutching or resistance.)

ATTACHMENT TO ...
Stream of Consciousness:
(Just let your mind think of things about the attachment. Write it down and see what you wrote or thought as wanting approval, wanting control or wanting to be safe or secure and then release the want.)

What advantage is it to me to _____ ?
What disadvantage is it to me to _____ ?
(Always put the same attachment in the blank space.)
1. Imagine never, ever being able to _____ .
(Put the attachment in the blank space and let go of clutching or resisting the feeling it brings up in your stomach or chest. Keep releasing until there are no more feelings in your stomach or chest.)

2. Could I let go of my entire attachment to _____ ?
(Put the attachment in the blank space and keep letting go until you can say "yes" 100% with no clutching or resistance.

AVERSION TO ...
Stream of Consciousness:
(Just let your mind think of things about the aversion. Write it down and see what you wrote or thought of as wanting approval, wanting control or wanting to be safe or secure and then release the want.)
What do I like about _____ ?
What do I dislike about _____?
(Always put the same aversion in the blank space.)

1. Imagine always _____ .
(Put the aversion in the blank space and let go of clutching or resisting the feeling it brings up in your stomach or chest. Keep releasing until there are no more feelings in your stomach or chest.)
2. Could I let go of my entire aversion to _____ ?
(Put the aversion in the blank space and keep letting go until you can say "yes" 100% with no clutching or resistance.)

Chapter 12

CHAPTER TWELVE

GETTING RID OF THE HABIT
OF BEATING YOURSELF UP

The moment the mind is right, the body is right.
--Lester Levenson

We all seem to have a habit of beating ourselves up. Some people do it to motivate themselves, others do it to control themselves. We do it for a variety of reasons--all of them done without discrimination and without realizing that we are storing up huge amounts of negative energy in our bodies. We are also storing up self-defeating programs which stop us from having the good things in life. This is where the famous "I don't deserve it" comes from. It's extremely important to rid oneself of this debilitating habit. So let's begin!

Let's do an attachment to disapproving of yourself and an aversion to disapproving of yourself or "beating yourself up."

And now let's ask one more of the "squeezing the lemon" questions. What we're doing is bringing up our subconscious mind, taking a look at our resistance, our clutching, and letting it go.

Imagine disapproving of yourself all the time. You can't stop. You're going to continue this forever. Tilt your head down and notice it brings up an unwanted energy and just allow it to pass through. And more. And even more. Put your hand on your feeling center (your stomach or chest area) and allow it to pass through. And more. And even more. One more time: Imagine disapproving of yourself forever. You can't stop. You're going to have to do it all the time. You're stuck with it. Allow that energy to come up in your stomach or chest area. Don't push it down. Allow it to come up and allow it to pass through. And more. And even more. Continue releasing until you have no more clutching in your feeling center.

And now, could you let go of your entire aversion to disapproving of yourself? Release anything that's stopping you from saying yes--a clutching, a resistance, an energy. Just allow that energy to come up and pass through. And more. And even more. And could you let go of your entire aversion to disapproving of yourself? Just allow that energy to come up and allow it to pass through. It's not good, it's not bad, it's just energy. Just phenomenon. Now you keep doing it until you can say yes 100%, in which case that entire aversion is gone.

74

ATTACHMENT TO DISAPPROVING OF YOURSELF

Now let's look at the attachment to disapproving of ourselves. If you keep disapproving of yourself, there must be some subconscious attachment to continuing this habit and some subconscious habit. So let's take a look at that by having you complete the attachment chart.

ATTACHMENT TO DISAPPROVING OF MYSELF
Stream of Consciousness:
(Just let your mind think of things about the attachment. Write it down and see what you wrote or thought of as wanting approval, wanting control, or wanting to be safe or secure and then release the want.)

What advantage is it to me to disapprove of myself?

_____

_____

_____

_____

What disadvantage is it to me to disapprove of myself?

_____

_____

_____

_____

1. Imagine never, ever being able to disapprove of myself again. (Let go of clutching or resisting the feeling it brings up in your stomach or chest. Keep releasing until there are no more feelings in your stomach or chest.)

2. Could I let go of my entire attachment to disapproving of myself? (Keep letting go until you can say yes 100% with no clutching or resistance.)

Stream of Consciousness:
(Just let your mind think of things about the attachment. Write it down and see what you wrote or thought as wanting approval, wanting control or wanting to be safe or secure and then release the want.)

What advantage is it to me to _____ ?

What disadvantage is it to me to _____ ?

(Always put the same attachment in the blank space.)

1.   Imagine never, ever being able to _____ .
(Put the attachment in the blank space and let go of clutching or resisting the feeling it brings up in your stomach or chest. Keep releasing until there are no more feelings in your stomach or chest.)

2.   Could I let go of my entire attachment to _____ ?
(Put the attachment in the blank space and keep letting go until you can say "yes" 100% with no clutching or resistance.

What advantage is it for you to disapprove of yourself? Make something up. Give me something silly. Could you see that as either wanting approval, wanting control or wanting to be safe and secure? And whichever want it brings up, could you just let it go? And more. And more.

And what disadvantages are there in you disapproving of yourself? Use your imagination and come up with something dumb or silly. Whatever it is, could you see it as either wanting approval, wanting control or wanting to be safe and secure? And whichever want it brings up, could you just let it go? And more. And more. And what's another advantage of disapproving of yourself? If the word none comes up, or I'm numb, see that as wanting approval, wanting control or wanting to be safe or secure or whatever you came up with. And whichever want was stirred up, could you let it go? The want equals lack, so just let it go.

And what's another disadvantage of disapproving of yourself? Whichever want that gets stirred up, could you just let it go? Whether it's a want of approval, control or being safe and secure, could you just let it go? And more. And more. Continue with this until you have no more advantages or disadvantages that come up. Then move on.

And now let's ask the "squeezing the lemon" question on the attachment side. Imagine never, ever, ever being able to disapprove of yourself again. You lost that ability. If that brings up an unwanted energy a clutching, a resistance either put your hand on your stomach or chest OR put your head down. Just allow that energy, which wants to leave, to come up and pass through. And more. And more. Don't try to understand the energy. Just let it go. You may surprise yourself in realizing you had a subconscious attachment to beating yourself up. It shows up through the clutching sensation in your feeling center.

One more time: Imagine never, ever being able to disapprove of yourself again. You lost that ability. See if there's any resistance, any clutching, any choking. Just allow it to come up and just allow it to pass through. Remember, it's not good, it's not bad and it's just phenomena energy passing through from your stomach or your chest area. And more. And even more.

And could you let go of your entire attachment to disapproving of yourself (or beating yourself up)? Any resistance to saying yes or any difficulty in saying yes?

This is only a habit. Consciously, we wouldn't do anything to hurt ourselves, but when we push this energy into the subconscious mind, it runs until we take it of our mind, much like deleting a computer file. So let's begin pulling it up and letting it go.

Suggestion: If you have a stronger aversion to something, it's a good idea to work on aversion first. But if you have a stronger attachment to something, then work on that first. Work on whichever is easier for you to stop, then work on the other.

My experience has usually been that most people have an aversion to dis-approving of themselves more than an attachment to it. They don't like the habit. They want to stop it. It's a desire to stop it. This is not necessarily so in every case, but it does occur in most instances. So let's start with an aversion to disapproving of yourself. Take out the chart on aversion to disapproving of your-self and complete it.

AVERSION TO DISAPPROVING OF MYSELF
Stream of Consciousness:
(Just let your mind think of things about the aversion. Write it down and see what you wrote or thought as wanting approval, wanting control, or wanting to be safe or secure and then release the want.)

What advantage is it to me to disapprove of myself?

_____

_____

_____

_____

What disadvantage is it to me to disapprove of myself?

_____

_____

_____

_____

1. Imagine disapproving of myself all the time. (Let go of clutching or resisting the feeling it brings up in your stomach or chest. Keep releasing until there are no more feelings in your stomach or chest.)

2. Could you let go of your entire aversion to disapproving of yourself? (Keep letting go until you can say yes 100% with no clutching or resistance.)

So what do you like about disapproving of yourself? Maybe that's the way you motivate yourself? Maybe you think it gets you going? Maybe you think you're lazy and you need that push to make things happen? So could you see whatever comes up as a wanting of approval, a wanting of control or a wanting to be safe and secure? And could you let go of either wanting approval, wanting control or wanting to be safe and secure? And could you let it go? And more.

And what don't you like about disapproving of yourself? And whatever comes up, could you see that as either wanting approval, wanting control, or wanting to be safe and secure? And could you let it go? And more. And even more.

Now what's something else you like about disapproving of yourself? Could you see that as either wanting approval, wanting control or wanting to be safe and secure? And could you either let go of either wanting approval, wanting control or wanting to be safe and secure? It's just an energy in your stomach or your chest area. Let go of clutching and allow that energy to just pass through. And more. And even more. And what don't you like about disapproving of yourself? Whatever answer that you get, could you see that as either wanting approval, wanting control or wanting to be safe and secure? And whichever want is stirred up, could you just let go of that want? That lacking feeling? Allow it to pass through? And more. And more.

And one more: What do you like about disapproving of yourself? Make something up. Give me something silly. "It's a habit. It feels good, I'm used to it," whatever. Or if you come up with the ever-popular "none", see that as either wanting control or wanting to be safe. And just let go of either wanting approval, wanting control or wanting to be safe and secure.

And what don't you like about disapproving of yourself? Whichever want it brings up, could you just let go of that lacking feeling? Could you allow it to pass through? And more. And even more. Keep going from each side to the next until you have no more likes or dislikes on the subject. Remember not to make an intellectual list of likes and dislikes without releasing on each item.

Now we're going to ask the "squeezing the lemon" question: Imagine disapproving of yourself all the time; you can't stop. Tilt your head down and notice that there's an unwanted energy there--a clutching, a resistance. And just allow this energy--which wants to leave--to come up and allow it to pass through...just like the oil wells in Kuwait. This energy wants to leave, so don't stop it...allow it to leave. It's just phenomenon. Just allow it to pass through. And more. And even more.

And now let's ask one more of the "squeezing the lemon" questions. What we're doing is bringing up our subconscious mind, taking a look at our resistance, our clutching, and letting it go.

Imagine disapproving of yourself all the time. You can't stop. You're going to continue this forever. Tilt your head down and notice it brings up an unwanted energy and just allow it to pass through. And more. And even more. Put your hand on your feeling center (your stomach or chest area) and allow it to pass through. And more. And even more. One more time: Imagine disapproving of yourself forever. You can't stop. You're gonna have to do it all the time. You're stuck with it. Allow that energy to come up in your stomach or chest area. Don't push it down. Allow it to come up and allow it to pass through. And more. And even more. Continue releasing until you have no more clutching in your feeling center.

And now, could you let go of your entire aversion to disapproving of yourself? Release anything that's stopping you from saying "yes"--a clutching, a resistance, an energy. Just allow that energy to come up and pass through. And more. And even more. And could you let go of your entire aversion to disapproving of yourself? Just allow that energy to come up and allow it to pass through. It's not good, it's not bad, it's just energy...just phenomenon. Now you keep doing it until you can say "yes" 100%, in which case that entire aversion is gone.

ATTACHMENT TO DISAPPROVING OF YOURSELF
Now let's look at the attachment to disapproving of ourselves. If you keep disapproving of yourself, there must be some subconscious attachment to continuing this habit...some subconscious habit. So let's take a look at that by having you complete the attachment chart.

Stream of Consciousness:
(Just let your mind think of things about the attachment. Write it down and see what you wrote or thought of as wanting approval, wanting control, or wanting to be safe or secure and then release the want.)

What advantage is it to me to disapprove of myself?

_____

_____

_____

79

What disadvantage is it to me to disapprove of myself?

1. Imagine never, ever being able to disapprove of myself again. (Let go of clutching or resisting the feeling it brings up in your stomach or chest. Keep releasing until there are no more feelings in your stomach or chest.)

Could I let go of my entire attachment to disapproving of myself?
(Keep letting go until you can say "yes" 100% with no clutching or resistance.)

What advantage is it for you to disapprove of yourself? Make something up. Give me something silly. Could you see that as either wanting approval, wanting control or wanting to be safe and secure? And whichever want it brings up, could you just let it go? And more. And more.

And what disadvantages are there in you disapproving of yourself? Use your imagination...come up with something dumb or silly. Whatever it is, could you see it as either wanting approval, wanting control or wanting to be safe and secure? And whichever want it brings up, could you just let it go? And more. And more.

And what's another advantage of disapproving of yourself? If the word "none" comes up, or "I'm numb," see that as wanting approval, wanting control or wanting to be safe or secure-or whatever you came up with. And whichever want was stirred up, could you let it go? The want equals lack, so just let it go.

And what's another disadvantage of disapproving of yourself? Whichever want that gets stirred up, could you just let it go? Whether it's a want of approval, control or being safe and secure, could you just let it go? And more. And more. Continue with this until you have no more advantages or disadvantages that come up. Then move on.

And now let's ask the "squeezing the lemon" question on the attachment side. Imagine never, ever, ever being able to disapprove of yourself again. You lost that ability. If that brings up an unwanted energy--a clutching, a resistance--either put your hand on your stomach or chest OR put your head down. Just allow that energy, which wants to leave, to come up and pass through. And more. And more. Don't try to understand the energy. Just let it go. You may surprise yourself in realizing you had a subconscious attachment to beating yourself up. It shows up through the clutching sensation in your feeling center.

One more time: Imagine never, ever being able to disapprove of yourself again. You lost that ability. See if there's any resistance, any clutching, any choking. Just allow it to come up and just allow it to pass through. Remember, it's not good, it's not bad...it's just phenomena--energy passing through from your stomach or your chest area. And more. And even more.

And could you let go of your entire attachment to disapproving of yourself? Any resistance to saying "yes" or any difficulty in saying "yes?"

This is only a habit. Consciously, we wouldn't do anything to hurt ourselves but when we push this energy into the subconscious mind, it runs until we take it out of our mind, much like deleting a computer file. So let's begin pulling it up and letting it go.

Suggestion: If you have a stronger aversion to something, it's a good idea to work on aversion first. But if you have a stronger attachment to something, then work on that first. Work on whatever is easier for you to stop, then work on the other.

My experience has usually been that most people have an aversion to disapproving of themselves more than an attachment to it. They don't like the habit. They want to stop it. It's a desire to stop it. This is not necessarily so in every case, but it does occur in most instances. So let's start with an aversion to disapproving of yourself. Take out the chart on aversion to disapproving of yourself and complete it.

Just get in touch with that energy, that clutching in your stomach or chest area, that resisting...and just let that energy go. And more. And even more.

And now let's ask one more of the "squeezing the lemon" questions. What we are doing is bringing up our subconscious mind and taking a look at our resistance, our clutching, and letting it go.

Imagine disapproving of yourself all the time. You can't stop. You're gonna continue this forever. Tilt your head down and notice it brings up an unwanted energy and just allow it to pass through. And more. And even more. Put your hand on your feeling center (your stomach or chest area) and allow it to pass through. And more. And even more. One more time: Imagine disapproving of yourself forever. You can't stop. You're going to have to do it all the time. You're stuck with it. Allow that energy to come up in your stomach or chest area. Don't push it down. Allow it to come up and allow it to pass through. And more. And even more. Continue releasing until you have no more clutching in your feeling center.

And now: could you let go of your entire aversion to disapproving of yourself? Release anything that's stopping you from saying "yes"--a clutching, a resistance, an energy. Just allow that energy to come up and pass through. And more. And even more. And could you let go of your entire aversion to disapproving of yourself? Just allow that energy to come up and allow it to pass through. It's not good, it's not bad, it's just energy...just phenomenon. Now you keep doing it until you can say "yes" 100%, in which case that entire aversion is gone.

Continue working on this on the "Attachment to Disapproving Yourself" and the "Aversion to Disapproving of Yourself" worksheets. You may want to work on this more deeply, or you may have cleaned it up. If this is the case, then fine. With no attachments and no aversions, you fall right into imperturbability. You are on your way to having abundance of everything

CHAPTER THIRTEEN

USING THE TECHNIQUE
TO IMPROVE YOUR HEALTH

"Desire is the cause of everything.
Any time you have any problem, there's desire behind it."
--Lester Levenson

HEALTH AND YOUR WELL-BEING

We have already touched upon important areas relating to your overall well-being, but now we will focus more on inner emotional stress that cause illnesses--or what is commonly known as "stress." The purpose of health and wealth, after all, is merely because we presume (and to some extent it is true) that they result in happiness. Happiness can be experienced directly, however, and on this level it is totally independent of health or wealth.

Let us take the situation of the average person and look at it objectively. To begin with, whatever happiness he or she thinks they have is extremely vulnerable. A chance remark, a critical comment, a lifted eyebrow, a car cutting into line ahead--all these are sufficient to blow the average person's happiness in an instant. The threat of a job loss, a feeling of threat to a relationship, a negative remark from a doctor, an impertinent cab driver--all are sufficient to blow most people's cool. Every time we suppress this energy (which is smaller than a photon particle), this negative energy stores up over the years and begins to press against the organs of the body, causing it to malfunction. As a result of negative feelings, thoughts and attitudes, as well as constant judgment and criticism of other people, the average person stores up this stress energy without realizing it. This energy causes the body to malfunction. Releasing this energy allows the body to heal itself, sometimes within moments.

Graduates of "The Abundance Course" report to us that they have released and cured allergies, asthma, arthritis, heart problems, back pain, limb pain, cancer, common colds, flu, hepatitis, epilepsy, AIDS, brain damage and more. When our body hurts, we all start to figure out how to get rid of this "dis-ease." By figuring it out, we unconsciously hold onto the very thing we are looking to get rid of. We keep trying different cures, practitioners, pills and modalities without much improvement. That is because we need to get rid of internal dis-ease. When we do, by directly releasing on them, the dis-ease disappears. Doctors know that a peaceful and positive mind is the best doctor of all. It can cure and fix anything in the body.

Furthermore, releasing can be instrumental in healing others. One of the graduates wrote to us: "Two weeks ago our son 'cracked up' at college and we had to pick him up. I called you and you said: There is no such thing as mental illness. Can you just let it go and let him be normal, healthy and whole with ease? I really latched on to the statement 'with ease?' and repeatedly said it in my mind even when the psychiatrist told us two days later that he was mentally ill, paranoid schizophrenic and would always need to be on medication. I did not give him the medication. I did take him to a homeopathic doctor that I knew and trusted. Within two days, he was beginning to act normal and now, two weeks later, he is fine!!!"

HERE IS WHAT SOME OF THE LEADING SCIENTISTS AND MEDICAL PRACTITIONERS WHO HAVE STUDIED "THE RELEASE® TECHNIQUE" HAVE TO SAY ABOUT ITS EFFECTIVENESS:

"I had several physical ailments including migraine headaches, diverticulitis, gout and severe hypoglycemia. The week after taking the course, I was scheduled for surgery. But within a few days after beginning to release, the surgical condition disappeared and never reappeared. My other physical problems cleared up. I believe these good effects are due to the stress reduction brought about by using the Method."

Dr. David Hawkins
Medical Director, The North Nassau Mental Health Center
Manhassett, NY

"In my experience, "The RELEASE® Technique" is simply the most effective way of reducing stress on both a personal and professional level. It constitutes a dramatic advance in the field of health and wellness."

Christopher Pruitt, M.D.
American Wellness Consultants

"I consider "The RELEASE® Technique" to be the best contribution to preventative medicine that I have seen in my 25 years of interest in the field. I am amazed at the simplicity of the training and its effectiveness."

John L. Kemeny, M.D.
Columbia University Medical School

"The Release Technique is different from anything I have ever done before. It works on a feeling level and allows people to eliminate negative emotions and thoughts. The Release Technique is so fast and effective because it goes directly to the heart of the problem...it's a shortcut for everyone who uses it."

Elliott Grumer, M.D.
Good Samaritan Hospital
Phoenix, AZ

"I have looked into other methods of stress management before finding the Release Technique, but have not discovered anything else so simple, powerful and rapidly effective. The most appealing features of The Method for me are the absence of an imposed belief system and the fact that people can use it completely on their own with great success."

Louis Ormont, Ph.D.
Psychology Department
Adelphi University

SCIENTIFIC STUDIES

Researchers David McClellan of Harvard University Medical School and Richard Davidson of The State University of New York have found that "The RELEASE® Technique" "stands out far beyond the rest for simplicity, efficiency, absence of questionable concepts and rapidity of observable results." These studies also reveal that individuals using "The RELEASE® Technique" show significant reduction in heart rate and diastolic blood pressure. With respect to short- versus long-term gain, the overall findings suggest that it is effective in promoting and maintaining stress reduction months after the training.

If you have a deficiency in your body, I suggest you try releasing on it. Releasing certainly will not hurt you in any way and, of course, if you can't release on it, you can always consult with a medical practitioner. When your body hurts, we start disapproving or beating up that part of the body, thus sending negative energy to the very part of the body we want to send positive energy to. Start reversing this habit by noticing the disapproving energy contained in your stomach or chest and putting the imaginary tube into the unwanted energy and releasing it. Then proceed to send that pain that is hurting (or deficient) positive energy by giving it approval. Some might say, "You want me to give my body approval? It hurts! I'm in pain!" But ask yourself, "Whose body is it that hurts?" That will help you discriminate that it is your body, not some ethereal body outside yourself. If it is your body or your pain, release it and give it approval. If you do that continually, your body will naturally correct itself.

The following releasing exercises will help you normalize your body and rid itself of the blockages which cause the discomfort. If you have a part of your body that isn't working properly, or you have pain or an uncomfortable feeling about it, check and see if you have been trying to figure out how to get rid of it (thus, holding it in your mind). Could you let go of figuring out how to get rid of it? You might as well, you haven't been able to get rid of it anyway. And could you let go of some more...and more? Could you let go of wanting to know what to do about it? And more? And more? And could you let go of wanting to know the answer? And more? And more? Could you let go of clutching about it? Notice there's a clutching feeling in your feeling center, your stomach or chest. And more, and more? Could you let go of resisting it, the energy in your stomach or chest area? And more? And more?

Now see if you have been disapproving of this disease or discomfort in you. By disapproving of it, you are sending negative energy to a place that is already a pocket of negative energy, and you're only making the situation worse. Could you let go of disapproving of it? And more? And more? So, could you give it some approval? By sending it positive energy, you allow the body to heal itself. Pain is like a doorbell ringing, saying "Please fix me." Your body is telling you to fix it. You can not fix it by sending your body negative energy. By doing this, you are only stopping the body from healing itself. So could you give your body some approval? Just because it's the smart thing to do? And more? And more?

Now keep looking for your disapproving of this "dis-ease." Every time you catch yourself beating your body up, let go. Then practice giving it approval. If you continually do this, the dis-ease will disappear.

Now let's do a releasing exercise on wellness. Then go on and do an attachment and aversion to health or that disease of a problem with your health exercise. You will find a "Releasing Stuckness" chart that will be very helpful in eliminating the stuckness about your health subject or any subject you may want to work on.

What is my NOW Feeling About Wellness?

Instructions:
Write down your NOW feelings about each topic, taking one topic at a time. Then trace that NOW feeling to either apathy, grief, fear, lust, anger or courageousness, acceptance and peace. Than see it as a wanting of approval, control or security and let it go to completion.

Once you have released the feeling completely check the *Let go?* column. When you have *let it go*, look back and see what the next feeling is about the topic. Do this until you feel at least courageousness about that topic, Then repeat the process with the next topic.

What is my NOW feeling about the condition of health?	Let go?	What is my NOW feeling about my physical health?	Let go?	What is my NOW feeling about exercise?	Let go?
I need to take better care of my body in terms of diet and exercise – fear	✓	*I should lose 10 pounds – Lust*	✓	*I need to work out more often – pride*	✓

*Did I completely let go?

What is my NOW Feeling About Wellness?

What is my NOW feeling about the condition of health?	Let go?	What is my NOW feeling about my physical health?	Let go?	What is my NOW feeling about exercise?	Let go?

*Did I completely let go?

ATTACHMENT TO HEALTH
Stream of Consciousness:
(Just let your mind think of things about the attachment. Write it down and see what you wrote or thought as wanting approval, wanting control, or wanting to be safe or secure and then release the want.)

What advantage is it to me to be healthy?

_____

_____

What disadvantage is to me to be healthy?

_____

_____

    1.   Imagine never, ever being able to be healthy. (Keep releasing until there are no more feelings in your stomach or chest.)

    2.   Could I let go of my entire attachment to health? (Keep letting go until you can say "yes" 100% with no clutching or resistance.)

AVERSION TO HEALTH
Stream of Consciousness:
(Just let your mind think of things about the aversion. Write it down and see what you wrote or thought of as wanting approval, wanting control or wanting to be safe and secure and then release the want.)

What do I like about being healthy?

_____

_____

What do I dislike about being healthy?

_____

_____

    1.   Imagine always being healthy. (Keep releasing until there are no more feelings in your stomach or chest.)

    2.   Could I let go of my entire aversion to health? (Keep letting go until you can say "yes" 100% with no clutching or resistance.)

Releasing Stuckness

Take a topic where you are experiencing stuckness (i.e. making a decision, a goal, an undesirable habit or behavior pattern, a troublesome relationship or situation, a recurring a feeling.

Start with one advantage, write it down, then write "wanting approval," "wanting to control," or "wanting security" next to is and release the NOW want completely. Check the *Let Go?* column.

Then go to one disadvantage, write it down, and go through the same steps. Go back to another advantage, repeating the same steps. Then do another disadvantage, then another advantage, then another disadvantage, so that you continue alternating the items and keep them balanced. If you can't come up with something, write "none" in that column and continue your releasing.

Topic: *Being Overweight*

What is the advantage to me?	Let go?	What is the disadvantage to me?	Let go?
I can eat what I want – wanting to control	✓	*My clothes don't fit – wanting approval*	✓
Keeps people away – wanting approval	✓	*I hate the way I look – wanting approval*	✓
I can just give up – wanting to control	✓	*People judge me – wanting approval*	✓

*Did I completely let go?

CHAPTER FOURTEEN

RELEASING AND RELATIONSHIPS; RELEASING AND SEXUAL RELATIONS

Love cannot be applied to one and not to another. It is impossible to love one and to hate another, for true love is unconditional. True love has no element of needing another or trying to control or possess another. True love's only desire is to make every other one happy.
--Lester Levenson

RELEASING AND RELATIONSHIPS

Because they are so intimately connected with our basic desires for love and security, relationships quickly bring up our innermost feelings. For that reason, they are extremely valuable, no matter whether the relationship is classified as good or bad. In the process of going free, everything is equally valuable. It is necessary to remind ourselves that feelings are programs; that is, they are learned reactions that have a purpose--and that purpose is directly related to achieving some end in the form of some effect on another person's feelings and, by doing so, to manipulate their behavior toward us and fulfill our own inner goals.

As we shall see, all emotions toward others involve the basic belief that we are incomplete within ourselves and, therefore, others are exploited and viewed as a means to an end. Although we may not be able to actually use the other person in the way we would like to, the utilization of the other person still occurs on the level of fantasy and expectation. We also discover that much of what we experience in a relationship is happening in our imagination only.

Before we examine the different emotions in relationships, we must first establish that love is a state of beingness, of oneness with another. It is NOT an emotion. It is NOT a feeling. Any emotion such as desire, resentment, revenge or jealousy, is changeable and transient, depending on the state of mind of the person experiencing it. It can be altered by a multitude of factors, may it be a change in the circumstances, alcohol or drugs. True love is pure and constant, unchanging. The kind of love which eventually vanishes or turns into a negative emotion was not really love in the first place. It was merely attachment, dependency, or possessiveness. Love is the only thing we do not need to release because lovingness equals beingness.

And now let us examine the consequences of the different emotions.

The negative feelings such as apathy, grief, fear, lust, anger and pride, take an enormous emotional toll on our inner selves, which often create physical illness. As if that was not bad enough, when we are feeling hateful and angry towards others, they inevitably reciprocate by avoiding or counterattacking us.

All negative energies are essentially forms of fear. Positive energies are essentially forms of love. The more we release, the higher we go. The higher we go the closer we come to total beingness, to pure love.

It is obvious that high states of consciousness have a profound effect on our relationships because one of the laws of consciousness is that like attracts like, and our inner states are actually radiated to others. We can positively affect others even from a distance because feelings are energy and energy gives off vibrations. We are like Sending and Receiving Stations. The more we love, the more we find ourselves surrounded by love. The replacement of a negative feeling by a higher one accounts for many miracles one can experience.

Releasing all emotions creates a miraculous shift.

A graduate of the Release Technique illustrated this by a story: "I was President of a small corporation with about fifty employees. We promoted a promising young man as head of one of the company's divisions. It turned out, however, that this man was very immature. Instead of reacting with gratitude and cooperation for all that was done for him, he reacted by becoming grandiose, demanding and somewhat paranoid. He stated he was going to barge into the next Board of Directors meeting and cause a big upset with his wild accusations and demands. Although these accusations could easily be refuted the whole situation was still an awful and painful experience to live through. For days I just plain hated this guy for all the trouble he was causing with his unfounded claims and threats. The day of the Board meeting I was driving along the parkway thinking angry thoughts about him. Suddenly I let go--I released on him totally. I started to see the frightened child in him and began to send him love. All my anxiety disappeared. I felt a sympathetic love for him when I looked at my watch; it was 12:30 p.m. When I got to the office my secretary said that this man walked into the office at the last minute and called off the whole thing. He said he changed his mind and realized he made a mistake. I asked her at what time he had walked into the office. She said she made particular note of the time as the Board meeting was soon to take place. She had looked at her watch when he made his announcement about his change of heart. The time was exactly 12:30 p.m."

The best way to facilitate harmony and satisfaction in relationships is to visualize lovingly the best possible outcome, making sure it is mutually beneficial, a win-win situation.

Release all negative feelings and merely hold the picture in mind. You can tell if you are really released if it is OK with you if it happens or if it doesn't.

One resistance to releasing is the illusion that if we let go of our wanting-ness that we won't get what we want. We will lose it if we don't keep pressing for it. The mind has the idea that the way to get a thing is to want it. Actually, if you examine the issue, you will see that events are due to decisions and choices based on our intentions. What we get is the result of these choices, even though they are unconscious rather than what we think we want. When we release the pressure of wantingness, we are clear to make wiser choices and decisions.

We think that our happiness depends on controlling events and that it is facts that upset us. Actually, it is our feelings and thoughts about these facts that are really the cause of the upset. Facts, in and of themselves, are neutral things. The power we give them is due to our attitude of acceptance or non-acceptance and our overall feeling state. If we get stuck in a feeling, it is because we still secretly believe that it will accomplish something for us. Therefore, I recommend you do some releasing on some of your relationships. You might do an attachment and aversion exercise on someone in your life, or you might do the stuckness exercise. Try it. You'll like it!

IMPROVING SEXUAL RELATIONS

Because of the wide availability of sexual material and opportunities for varied sexual experience, most people nowadays consider themselves rather sexually liberated. This liberation is primarily intellectual and behavioral. However, there still exists a great deal of emotional and experiential limitation, as well as sensory restriction. All experience takes place within consciousness itself so that sexual experience, like any other, is determined by one's overall level of awareness and inner freedom.

The degree to which one's sexual experience has been restricted becomes apparent the more one releases on feelings. When one is totally released on sexuality, it is like adding a third dimension to what was before a two-dimensional experience. As one woman put it, "It's like I used to hear just violins. Then a cello was added, and then a flute, and so on, so that now the experience is totally full and comprehensive."

Besides the greater emotional pleasure of freedom of expression, there is a change in the sensory experience itself. To most people (men especially), sexual excitation and orgasmic pleasure are primarily a genital sensation. As one gets freer, the locale of the orgasm begins to expand and spread to the whole pelvis and abdomen, the legs and arms...the whole body. After this accomplishment, there is often a plateau that follows and then, suddenly and unexpectedly, the orgasmic location expands beyond the body--as though the space around the body was having the orgasm instead of the person. Ultimately, there is no limitation of the orgasm. It seems to expand into infinity and be experienced from no particular center or locale. It is as if there is no individual person present. The orgasm is experiencing itself.

This expansion is facilitated by becoming aware that the facial grimacing and breath-holding are restrictions due to fear of loss of control and attempts to limit the experience. If one looks for any clutching or resistance during any sexual encounter, the fear will become conscious and can be released. Ultimately, your experience will be greatly enhanced.

Sexuality loses its compulsiveness because freedom means not just freedom to indulge, but freedom not to have sex or orgasm. When one is released, they are not run by the desire for the orgasm. This releases creative experiencing and awareness because the mind is not focused on the orgasm itself. To be free from the domination of the desire for orgasm allows sexual experiences (or anything you release on) to have a greater freedom to do or not to do them.

The freer one gets, the more one is motivated by lovingness rather than by desire for gratification. This change of motivation from wanting this in hunger to the sharing of pleasure and happiness brings about major changes in the nature of sexual relationships. The intimacy with another is more encompassing and pleasurable. There is greater attunement to the other person's sexuality and intuitive fulfillment of each other's styles and satisfactions. One couple expressed it as follows: "It is as though we just witness what our bodies are doing. It is as though we are the space in which it is all happening. As soon as one of us has a desire or fantasy, the other automatically--and without even thinking--moves in to the acting out of that fantasy. It is as though we are psychically connected. We got that way by releasing on our inner feelings about our fantasies and how we thought the other might react. There is greater variation and frequency, also. It used to be mainly Friday and Saturday nights. Now we make love for days at a time and go for weeks without it. It is always new. It is never the same. Amazingly, it just keeps getting better and better. Each orgasm is better than the last, and yet often we are so satisfied with the lovemaking that we don't even bother to have an orgasm. If it happens, it's OK and it's OK if it doesn't. I guess that's what being free really means."

At a releasing workshop of graduates, another man said, "I never really realized before how much sex ran my relationships. It was really compulsive. I was always afraid I would miss out on a sexual opportunity. If sex with a partner wasn't available, it was the same way with masturbation. I didn't want to miss out on the opportunity for pleasure. Now my pattern is more variable; in fact, now I have no pattern. When it happens, it happens and it's great when it does. When it doesn't, I don't even think about it. I used to have sex on my mind all the time. Girls would usually say no. But now that I really don't care that much about it, they all either suggest it or say yes if I ask. I find now I am concerned about them instead of me. I see that before I was really just using them for my own selfish ends and, intuitively, I knew it. Now I feel a lot of love for women. I really care about their welfare and happiness, even if it's only a one-night stand. What a relief not to have to lie anymore."

From the example above, it is clear that there is a change in consciousness from lack to abundance. A self-centered person is angry and frustrated and feels deprived. The more loving they become, the more they receive what they are giving and find that we are all surrounded by love and opportunities for loving involvements. One woman said, "I was always overweight and not good looking. All through my life, I envied and hated sexually attractive women. I got to hate men, too, because they avoided me. I was full of self-pity. I even tried psychotherapy, but I quit when it became apparent he was more interested in his attractive young women patients than he was in me. I did est and at least got over my self-pity and depression and got a better job, but men still weren't interested in me. Then I heard about 'The RELEASE® Technique' and took the basic course. Within a week, I had a date. I was so excited, I even lost my appetite. We had a great time! Then, all of a sudden, I saw the secret. I was giving love instead of looking for it. My whole life has changed now. When I enter a room, I see all the lonely, love-starved men. They look just the way I used to, so I really know what they are feeling, as well as what to say to them and how to express myself. I put myself in their place and watch them as their hearts melt. I used to scare them away because I was so hungry. Get that? Hungry! Yeah, that was my problem. Now I feel full and I share that fullness and share what I have learned. I know so many men I haven't time to eat anymore. I have lost 35 pounds in one year. I never even dieted. I just lost interest. I guess it is because I am getting gratified in a way now that really means something to me. Maybe I am a little wild with the newness of it, but I'll settle down before long. There is one guy I'm really interested in right now."

Later, the same woman said, "I see why you can't cure poverty with money. It's a state of consciousness. I see why the poorer get poorer and the richer get richer. It's what you are holding. It's the direction in which you are going. I surely am glad I changed direction. I could have ended up bitter and alone and died prematurely. Now I even have a new car. One of my boyfriends sold used cars and I got a real deal. Before I would have been suspicious and figured it was a crooked deal or something like that. Now I am more open and trusting."

Sexuality, then, joins in our overall state of consciousness. As we let go of fear and limitations, that area of our life expands and becomes ever more gratifying, and yet not necessary. Freedom and creativity replace compulsiveness and limitation. The pleasure of communion and non-verbal understanding replaces the former self-centered drive for relief from tension and the limited

Chapter 14

goal of sexual pleasure and ego inflation. The secret, as the woman above stated, is in the awareness that when we seek to give instead of to get, all our own needs are automatically fulfilled.

CHAPTER FIFTEEN

RESPONSIBILITY

The worst thing to do is to suppress a desire, any desire. When it is suppressed, from that moment on, it will try to express itself. Recognizing it does not mean we must try to satisfy it, but does prevent suppressing it.
--Lester Levenson

Now we are going to look at responsibility. Lester said that by taking responsibility for everything that goes on in our lives, we could open our flow to abundance. If we don't do it, we are out of control. If we do it, we're in control.

So let's just take a look at some of the things that we can do in preparation for taking a look at responsibility. I want you to think about having all the abundance in the world. What would you do? Would you take a trip? Would you buy a big house? Would you tell your boss to drop dead? Would you get rid of your spouse? Would you get a new spouse? Would you buy an airplane? A new car? Whatever it is, take a look at that and see if it brings up a wanting of approval, wanting of control or a wanting to be safe and secure.

Now think of something else you'd do if you had all the abundance in the world. Does that bring up a wanting of approval, wanting of control or wanting to be safe and secure? Now what else would you do if you had all the abundance in the world? Where would you go? What would you do? How would you act? What would you buy? Whatever gets stirred up, could you see that as wanting approval, control or safety? Now whichever want gets stirred up, could you let go of that want...that lacking feeling? And more. And even more. And what else would you do if you had all the abundance in the world? Does that bring up a wanting of approval, control or safety? Whichever want gets stirred up, could you just let it go? And what else would you do if you had all the abundance in the world? Where would you go, how would you act, who would you be with? What business would you be in? Would you retire? Would you take a trip to Europe? Around the world? Buy a house for your parents? Whatever. Whatever that brings up, could you see it as either a wanting of approval, control or safety? And whichever want that gets stirred up, could you just let go of that want? Let go of the wanting of approval, wanting of control or wanting of safety--or just an unwanted energy. Just allow it to come up and pass through. And more. And more.

Now what else would you do if you had all the abundance in the world? And whichever answer you have, could you see that as either a wanting of approval, control or safety? And whatever it is, could you just let go of that want? And more. And even more.

FIND OUT WHAT'S IN YOUR WAY

Now ask yourself what's in the way of you having abundance? What's in the way of you having money? Are you guilty? Do you feel you don't deserve it? Is it that you're not in the right place and you're into trying to figure it out? What's in the way? Let's examine that.

Whichever thought or feeling you have, could you see that as a wanting approval, control or safety? And could you let go of any or all of these feelings? And what else is in the way of you having abundance? Whichever want it brings up, could you see that as a wanting of approval, control or safety? And could you let go of these feelings? And whatever's in the way, whatever it is, could you see that as a wanting of approval, control or safety? And could you let it go?

At this point, stop and take a plain piece of paper out. Write down what you'd do if you had all the abundance in the world and then see each idea you come up with as a wanting of approval, control or safety. Whatever your answer is, just let go of either wanting approval, control or safety and then take a look at what's in the way of you having this thing. See if it brings up an unwanted energy, a resistance, a clutching or just plain wanting of approval, control or safety...and just let it go!

When you've finished with this exercise, we can continue forward.

RESPONSIBILITY

Taking responsibility is a powerful way of creating abundance in your life, as well as accelerating your releasing. The following quote from Lester describes how you can start creating and taking responsibility in your life.

"If you want one partial key for quickly reaching the Goal, I would recommend that you take full responsibility for everything that happens to you. We have lost sight of our mastership and have deluded ourselves into thinking that we are victims in a world that controls us, that pushes us around. It isn't so! We are causing what is happening to us by giving power, our power, to the external world. If you want to regain your control, you must take full responsibility.

How to regain our control? Examine your thinking and correct it. Develop the habit of honest introspection by asking yourself, "Wherein did I cause this to happen to me?' and holding it until the thought that caused the happiness comes out of the subconscious into the conscious plane. Then you recognize your mastership, that you caused that pleasant or unpleasant experience to happen to you. The more you will do this, the easier it becomes and the more able you become until, finally, you recognize that you were always the master."

--Lester Levenson

Fill in the blanks below. Write down whatever comes up and release it without censoring what you discover. Be open to seeing your underlying pattern or program about abundance. Take responsibility, but let go of beating yourself up. By taking responsibility, you can take control of what happens to you in your world. If you did it, you can change it. If you feel, "I didn't do it, it happened to me," you're stuck and you have to wait for something or someone outside of yourself to change--you become a victim.

WHEREIN DID I CAUSE MY LACK OF ABUNDANCE?
(Sit quietly until the answer comes. Write it down and keep releasing until you are 100% released about it.)

_____

_____

_____

_____

_____

_____

_____

_____

_____

_____

Chapter 15

CHAPTER SIXTEEN

THE MIND AND HOW IT WORKS

"Nervousness is caused by wanting two opposing things at the same time, one consciously and the other subconsciously. The battle is resolved when you make the subconscious desire conscious. On the other hand, if you know what you are, there will be no conflicts. You can do that through seeking. It is not necessary to understand the negative. It is far better to be positive. Be Your Self."
--Lester Levenson

THE MAP OF CONSCIOUSNESS

As you can see on the following page, the Map of Consciousness consists of a wedge shaped diagram divided into three broad bands, each of which corresponds to one of three states of consciousness. At the base is the state entitled "Body." To the left is the phrase "Extremely Limited You". This state is where many of us spend a great deal of time. It is one in which we experience ourselves as primarily defined by the boundaries of our physical being. It is the lowest of the three states and is identified by a very active mind that spends a lot of time thinking about things and doing very little. It is also a stage in which there are isolated moments of pleasure in a landscape that includes a lot of confusion, procrastination, sorrow and pain.

The second stage is entitled "Mind/Separation." To the left is the phrase "Limited You". This stage is characterized by a less frantic mind, fewer thoughts and some direct knowing. Life lived from this perspective is characterized by a general condition of well-being and happiness punctuated by moments of extreme doubt, sorrow and pain. Here, one is identified with the mind and ego. It is a higher and more empowered state than the first, but still this state is characterized by a lot of effort and "doingness."

The top stage is entitled "The Natural State." This is the all-knowing, all powerful, abundant, imperturbable stage. To the left is the phrase "Real You" and below that the word "Beingness." This is the free natural state Lester and other wise beings have described. It is a state without limit and boundary, one in which identification with the limits of body and mind have been dropped and one discovers the joy and peace of beingness. It is also that natural state in which one can manifest true success, well-being and lasting abundance.

MAP OF CONSCIOUSNESS CHART

The Real You
The Unlimited You
Beingness

All knowing, no thinking, intuitive only, oneness, no problems, quiet only, solutions, yes, I can, abundance of everything, havingness, no lacking, open, easy, no effort, no clutching

- Peace
- Acceptance
- Courageousness

The Unreal You
The Limited You

Questions, confusion, doubts, thinking I'm releasing, no trust, no satisfaction, desires, problems, struggles, I can'ts lies, effort, clutching

- Pride
- Anger
- Lust
- Fear

The Extremely
Limited You

Body hurts, tired, sick, headaches, sleepy, no energy

- Fear
- Grief
- Apathy

BODY

DEAD

We include this Map of Consciousness at this point because we want you to see graphically what happens as you begin to let go of negative thoughts, feelings and emotions--when you begin to move beyond the concepts of limitation into your natural state of beingness. I invite you to refer to it from time to time. You may even want to make a copy of it and hang it somewhere. It is a valuable graphic way to envision the goal you can achieve by using "The RELEASE® Technique".

When you experience your natural state, you change only in identity and point of view. Results: Imperturbability, tranquility, serenity and abundance of everything.

Now let's look at what Lester had to say about the mind:
"The mind is simply the sum total composite of all thoughts."
"The mind becomes habitual."
"The subconscious mind is merely the thoughts we are not looking at now."

That's exactly what we've been doing. We've been pulling them up, making ourselves conscious of it and then releasing them. The subconscious mind is running us, making us the victims of habit. By discriminating, we take a look at our feelings, our subconscious thoughts, and just release them.

You may have noticed that sometimes when you're doing advantages and disadvantages the same answer comes up on both sides. Have you noticed that? No wonder we're fighting ourselves. By releasing on both sides, we open up the flow and can move on freely with the inner clutching that often goes on when we are in conflict or confusion.

The direction is to still the mind. Quiet the mind and you'll see your infinity right there. The more you quiet the mind, the more you feel the self and the better you feel. You feel as good as your mind is quiet.

By now, you may be noticing that you've been feeling quieter and quieter and nicer and nicer. That is the real you, that beautiful table covered up with dust that we spoke about earlier. You're beginning to see the real you.

In your imagination, you have written and projected a cinema show of acts, actors and audience on a screen and have lost sight of the fact that it is all in your imagination, your mind. Discover this and you'll discover the absolute truth.

Mind distraction is the wanting more of the things of the world than the self.

A thought is an assumption of lack causing a wish to fulfill it.

Once you see what the mind is, you won't be subject to it anymore.

The power of the mind is almost infinite; when there is only one thought, all that power is right there.

The more you eliminate the mind, the more peaceful you feel.

All minds are influencing each other. We're like sending and receiving signals. Whatever you think about someone, you might as well tell them about it, for you are sending a receiving signal over to them and they are picking it up. We call it a "good vibe" or a "bad vibe." So I recommend that you release all the judgments you have and the thinking you have toward somebody, like somebody, and let it go.

HOW TO BE CLEAR AT ALL TIMES

Now let's take a look at this figuring it out business once more on a deeper level. It's habit, but by now, hopefully, you can see that figuring it out is the home of confusion. If you need to figure something out, it means you don't have an answer and, therefore, you start spinning around in your mind, asking it for the answer. If it doesn't have an answer, we tend to keep asking it anyway. That's because of habit and lack of discrimination on our part. Now I'm not talking about not having an answer. I'm not talking about being stupid. I'm talking about letting go of wanting the answer and having the answer.

Remember that wanting and having are opposites. Every time you engage your mind and throw it into wanting to figure it out, you're really engaging your mind and calling up what you have previously recorded in your mind. If that answer is not there, naturally, your mind is going to tell you, "I don't know what you're talking about."

And then, since we think the mind is the only place that can give us an answer, we start beating it up for not giving us an answer. The mind, like a computer, can only give back what you have previously experienced and recorded. So most people are living in the past. By constantly relying on the mind for all their answers, they stay stuck in old answers instead of getting new answers from a higher place. When you ask the mind to think about money, it's going to give you whatever you previously have experienced with regard to money. When you think about relationships, it's going to give you whatever you have on relationships. If you're worried about the future, it's going to bring up what you did in the past and cause you to be thinking about what happened in the past and, therefore, you think you're in the future. However, you're just relying on the past information or experiences. Be here now. Be clear, just release all those feelings and thoughts and you'll be clear as a bell.

So let's take a look at this attachment and aversion to "figuring it out." See the chart on the following page before continuing.

ATTACHMENT TO FIGURING THINGS OUT
Stream of Consciousness:
(Just let your mind think of things about the attachment. Write it down and see what you wrote or thought as wanting approval, wanting control or wanting to be safe or secure and then release the want.)

What advantage is it to me to figure things out?

_____

_____

_____

_____

What disadvantage is it to me to figure things out?

_____

_____

_____

_____

1.   Imagine never being able to figure things out ever again. (Let go of clutching or resisting the feeling it brings up in your stomach or chest. Keep releasing until there are no more feelings in your stomach or chest.)

2.   Could I let go of my entire aversion to figuring things out? (Keep letting go until you can say "yes" 100% with no clutching or resistance.)

Referring to the foregoing chart, let's walk through the process. First, do a stream of consciousness on your attachment to figuring things out. Release on it until you are clear on it. Now let's move on to advantages.

Now what advantage is it for you to figure things out? One advantage. Can you see that as wanting approval, wanting control or wanting to be safe? And whichever want it stirs up, could you let go of either wanting approval, wanting control or wanting to be safe? Now again, I'm not telling you NOT to have an answer, I'm telling you to let go and HAVE an answer.

What disadvantage is it for you to figure things out? Does that bring up a wanting of approval, control or safety? And what's another advantage to figuring things out? Does that stir up a wanting of approval, control or safety? Whichever answer you have, could you let go of either wanting approval, control or safety? And what's another disadvantage of figuring things out? Whichever thought or feeling it stirs up, could you see that thought or feeling as either wanting approval, control or safety? Whichever want that is stirred up, could you let it go? And more. And more. And what's another advantage of figuring things out? Could you see that as either wanting approval, control or safety? And could you let go of wanting these things? What disadvantage is it for you to figure things out? Is there a wanting of approval, control or safety? And could you let go of any or all of these feelings?

Now what's another disadvantage of you figuring things out? Does that bring up a wanting of approval, control or safety? Now whichever want it brings up, could you just let it go? And what advantage is it of yours to figure things out? Does that bring up a wanting of approval, control or safety? Whichever want it stirs up, could you just let it go? And what disadvantage is it for you to figure things out? Does that bring up a wanting of approval, control or safety? Could you let that want go? And more. And even more. Keep going back and forth until you're clean on it and then move on.

Now let's ask the "squeezing the lemon" question: Imagine never, ever, ever being able to figure things out again. You've lost the ability. Now see if that brings up a clutching, a resistance, an unwanted energy in your stomach or chest area...and just allow that energy to come up and allow it to pass through. Let it go so you can have the answers--different answers, not the same ones. Imagine never being able to figure things out again. You've lost the ability. Just let the energy come up and just allow it to pass through. It's not good, it's not bad--it's just phenomena passing through. And more...and even more. Imagine never ever being able to figure things out again. Just let the energy come up and just allow it to pass through.

Sometimes people at this point start to feel tired. If you're feeling tired or restless, notice that there's an unwanted energy in your stomach or your chest area or see it as either wanting approval, wanting control or wanting to be safe. And just let that energy leave. And more. And even more.

Now let's continue:

Imagine never ever being able to figure things out again. Just allow that energy to come up...just allow it to pass through. Each time you let go, you're moving towards imperturbability--quieting the mind, becoming more and more powerful, becoming more and more positive. Take a check and see if that isn't so.

Imagine never ever being able to figure things out again. You've lost the ability. Just let this energy come up and just allow it to pass through. It's just resistance. And more. And more. Continue on until you've totally released and are no longer resisting or clutching when you read the "squeezing the lemon" question. Now ask yourself, "Could I let go of my entire attachment to figuring things out?" And more...and even more. Continue on until you can say yes 100%.

AVERSION TO FIGURING THINGS OUT
Stream of Consciousness:
(Just let your mind think of things about the aversion. Write it down and see what you wrote or thought as wanting approval, wanting control or wanting to be safe and secure and then release the want.)

What do I like about figuring things out?

_____

_____

_____

_____

What don't I like about figuring things out?

_____

_____

_____

_____

1.   Imagine always figuring things out...everything. And you can't stop. (Let go of clutching or resisting the feeling it brings up in your stomach or chest. Keep releasing until there are no more feelings in your stomach or chest.)

2.   Could I let go of my entire aversion to figuring things out? (Keep letting go until you can say "yes" 100% with no clutching or resistance.)

Referring to the chart above, let's now look at the aversion to figuring things out. What do you like about figuring things out? Does that bring up a feeling of wanting approval, wanting control or wanting to be safe? And whichever want that it brings up, could you let go of either wanting approval, wanting control or wanting to be safe? And what don't you like about figuring things out? Does that bring up a wanting of approval, control or safety? Whichever want it is, could you just let it go?

And what do you like about figuring things out? Does that bring up a wanting of approval, control or safety? And could you let go of any or all of these wants? And what don't you like about figuring things out? Does that bring up a wanting of approval, control or safety? And could you just let go of that want? And what do you like about figuring things out? Does that bring up a wanting of approval, control or safety? And could you let go of it? Could you just let it go? And what don't you like about figuring things out? Does that bring up a wanting of approval, control or safety? And could you let go of any or all of these wants? Could you just let it go? And more...and more? Keep releasing until you are clean on it and then move on.

And now let's ask the "squeezing the lemon" question: Imagine always figuring things out--everything. You can't stop. You're going to have to do it for the rest of your life. See if that brings up a clutching, a resistance, an unwanted energy in your stomach or chest area. Put your head down, put your hand on your stomach or chest area and just allow that energy to pass through. And more. And even more. Imagine always figuring things out--everything. You can't stop. Just allow that energy, that resistance, to come up...and just let it pass through. And more. And more.

Each time we let go, we're moving closer and closer toward imperturbability. Take a check and see if that isn't so. Become calmer and quieter.

Imagine always figuring things out--everything. You can't stop. It brings up a resistance. Just allow that energy to come up. And more. And even more. Keep releasing until you're 100% clear on it and there is no more clutching. Then move on.

And could you let go of your entire aversion to figuring things out? If there's any resistance to saying yes, could you just let it go? Put your head down and let go of resisting. And more. And even more. Anything in the way of you saying "yes"? See if it brings up an unwanted energy and just allow it to pass through. And more...and even more. Could you let go of your entire aversion to figuring things out? And more...and even more. Do this until you can say yes 100%.

As you get clearer and clearer and more and more discriminating about a habit of figuring things out, you will begin to see that you constantly will be moving toward having the answers--rather than having the OLD answers. Just let go and find out.

CHAPTER SEVENTEEN

HOW TO RID YOURSELF OF WORRY

"The more you quiet your mind, the more you feel the Self--and the better you feel. You feel as good as your mind is quiet."
--Lester Levenson

Now we're going to continue eliminating all the obstacles in the way of us having abundance. And one of the big obstacles we have in life is a thing called "worrying." Does anybody like to worry? No, I suspect not. But it's a habit, so we're going to do attachments and aversion to worrying. The goal is to eliminate this nasty habit forever. Worrying stops us because we are holding in mind what we don't want. However, we continue to do it because it's a habit. So let's do an aversion to worrying because I have found that people usually have a bigger aversion than attachment to worrying. That's not necessarily so all the time, but let's just start with the aversion to begin our investigation.

ATTACHMENT TO WORRYING
Stream of Consciousness:
(Just let your mind think of things about the attachment. Write it down and see what you wrote or thought as wanting approval, control or safety. Then release the want.)

What advantage is it to me to worry?

_____

_____

_____

_____

What disadvantage is it to me to worry?

_____

_____

_____

_____

1.   Imagine never, ever being able to worry again. (Let go of clutching or resisting the feeling it brings up in your stomach or chest. Keep releasing until there are no more feelings in your stomach or chest.)

2.   Could I let go of my entire attachment to worrying? (Keep letting go until you can say "yes" 100% with no clutching or resistance.)

So what do you like about worrying? Does that bring up a wanting of approval, a wanting of control or a wanting to be safe? Could you let go of any or all of these wants? And what don't you like about worrying? Make something up. Use your imagination. So what if it makes no sense? We wouldn't necessarily consciously do anything destructive to ourselves, but we continue doing it out of habit and lack of discrimination. What we are doing is digging up the subconscious mind and letting it go. So, what do you like about worrying? Make something up. Make up something stupid. Use your imagination. Does that thought or feeling provoke a wanting of approval, control or safety? And could you let go of any or all of these wants? And more...and more...and even more. And what don't you like about worrying? Does that bring up a wanting of approval, control or safety? Could you let go of any or all of these wants? And what do you like about worrying? Again, keep digging deeper. Make something up; use your imagination. Does that stir up a wanting of approval, control or safety? And could you let these go?

And what don't you like about worrying? Does that bring up a wanting of approval, control or safety? Could you let go of either wanting approval, control or safety? And what do you like about worrying? Does that stir up a wanting of approval, control or safety? Could you just let it go, whichever feeling it stirs up? And what don't you like about worrying? Does that stir up a wanting of approval, control or safety? And whichever feeling it stirs up, could you just let it go? Wanting approval, control or safety and security--these are lacking feelings, so let them go.

Once more: What do you like about worrying? It's just a subconscious habit. A lot of people are protecting themselves with fear. That's like jumping into a swimming pool while holding onto a bag of cement and thinking it's going to help you float. So could you let go of protecting yourself with fear and with worry? And more. And more. So what do you like about worrying? Does that stir up a feeling of wanting approval, control or safety? Could you let go of these feelings? And what don't you like about worrying? Does that stir up a feeling of wanting approval, control or safety? Could you let go of these feelings, too?

And one more time: what do you like about worrying? Does that stir up a wanting of approval, control or safety? And could you let go of either wanting approval, control or a feeling of being safe and secure? And what don't you like about worrying? Does that stir up a wanting of approval, control or safety? And could you let go of these wants? And more. And more. And even more. Keep releasing until you are clear on both sides. Then move on.

AVERSION TO WORRYING
Stream of Consciousness:
(Just let your mind think of things about the aversion. Write it down and see what you wrote or thought as wanting approval, wanting control or wanting to be safe or secure and then release the want.)

What do I like about worrying?

_____

_____

_____

Is that wanting approval, wanting control, wanting to be safe? Couyld you let go of either wanting approval, wanting control, or wanting to be safe? Keep looking at this area and keep releasing until it is gone.

What don't I like about worrying?

_____

_____

_____

Is that wanting approval, wanting control, wanting to be safe? Couyld you let go of either wanting approval, wanting control, or wanting to be safe? Keep looking at this area and keep releasing on this until there is no more.

And now let's ask the "squeezing the lemon" question. Imagine always worrying...forever. You can't stop. Now that will probably create a clutching, resistance or unwanted energy in your stomach or chest. Can you put your head down and allow this energy to come up? Welcome it up. Let go of resisting it. Let go of clutching. Look for it. Imagine always worrying...forever. You can't stop. Just allow that energy to come up. Let it pass through. And more. And more. And even more. Imagine always worrying forever, not being able to stop. Whichever want or unwanted energy it stirs up, just allow it to come up and pass through. And more. And more. And even more. And could you let go of your entire aversion to worrying? Anything stopping you from saying "yes," put your head down, disengage it and allow that energy to come up and pass through. And more. And more. And even more. Keep releasing until there is no more clutching...and then move on.

And could you let go of your entire aversion to worrying? Just allow that energy to come up and just allow it to pass through. And more. And even more. Could you let go of your entire aversion to worrying? Anything stopping you from saying "yes?" Look for the clutching, resistance, unwanted energy and just allow it to come up and allow it to pass through. And more. And more. And even more. Continue with this question until you can say yes 100%.

Right now, take a look and see if there's any more worrying aspects you might want to look at and when you're ready, you can move on to attachment to thinking.

ATTACHMENT TO THINKING
Stream of Consciousness:
(Just let your mind think of things about the attachment. Write it down and see what you wrote or thought as wanting approval, wanting control or wanting to be safe or secure and then release the want.)

What advantage is it to me to think?

_____

_____

_____

_____

What disadvantage is it to me to think?

_____

_____

_____

_____

_____

So what advantage is it for you to think? Does that bring up a wanting of approval, a wanting of control or a wanting to be safe? Now whichever want it brings up, could you just let it go? Whether it's the wanting of approval, control or safety? Now what disadvantage is it to you to think? Make something up. Use your imagination. Does that bring up a wanting of approval, a wanting of control or a wanting to be safe? And whichever want it is, could you just let it go? Either the wanting of approval, wanting control or the wanting to be safe? Now what's another advantage of you thinking? Does that bring up a wanting of approval, a wanting of control or a wanting to be safe, secure and to survive? Could you let go of any or all of these wants? And more. And more. And more. And what disadvantage is it for you to think? Does that bring up a wanting of approval, control or safety? And more. And more. And more.

1.   Imagine never, ever being able to think. (Let go of clutching or resisting the feeling it brings up in your stomach or chest. Keep releasing until there are no more feelings in your stomach or chest.)
2.   Could I let go of my entire attachment to thinking? (Keep letting go until you can say "yes" 100% with no clutching or resistance.)

TAKING A LOOK AT AUTOMATIC THINKING
Now let me just talk a little bit about the process of thinking. We're learning how to master our minds so the mind becomes our servant instead of us having to listen to it all the time automatically. And that's what we're doing. So I'm not suggesting that we not think anymore. I'm suggesting that we master our mind and its thinking ability so we can be in charge of the mind instead of the mind being in charge of us.

One of Lester's favorite movies was "2001: A Space Odyssey". If you remember the movie, the computer called HAL 9000 took over the spaceship and killed everyone aboard in an attempt to take over. Keir Dullean (Dave), the remaining astronaut, was almost killed...pushed out of the spaceship by HAL. Somehow or other, he crawls back in the ship. Then the computer, HAL, starts talking to him: "Hold it a minute, you need me. Who's going to run this spaceship when you're sleeping? I'm sorry, I didn't mean it. I didn't mean to do anything wrong. I didn't mean to kill the other astronauts." But Dave keeps walking toward the computer and pulls all the tapes out. And HAL goes quiet as the tapes are removed. Then Dave takes over the spaceship. Basically, that's what happens with us and our minds. We forget who's in charge. We don't have to listen to all that worry and all that negativity and stuff like that. We can master our mind and let it become our servant instead of the other way around. So, by having discrimination about thinking, we get clearer and we know in which direction we should move. With this in mind, let's continue examining our thinking process and examine the mind and begin to master it--by pulling out its tapes.

ADVANTAGE TO THINKING
So what advantage is it for you to think? Does that bring up a wanting of approval, control or safety? Whichever want that gets stirred up, could you let it go? And what disadvantage is it for you to think? Make something up. Use your imagination. Could you see that as wanting approval, control or safety? And whichever want that gets stirred up, could you just let it go? Could you let go of wanting approval, control or safety? And what's another advantage to thinking? Does that bring up a wanting of approval, control or safety? And could

you let any of those go? And what disadvantage is there to thinking? Does it bring up a want of approval, control or safety? And whichever want gets stirred up, could you just let it go? And what's another advantage in thinking? Could you see that as a want of approval, control or safety? And could you let any or all of those go? Keep going back and forth until you are clear on any advantages and disadvantages. Then move on.

Now, what happened originally is the mind was supposed to be used to be our servant. It was supposed to help us remember names, faces, places and various things like that. Instead, it kind of took over and the servant became the master of the house. Now what we're doing is taking back control. We're taking charge so that you'll be able to adjust what your thinking is, what to use it on and prevent terror from it. You won't have to listen to it in a negative way. And that's what we're examining.

So imagine never, never, ever being able to think again. Now put your head down and see if it brings up an unwanted energy, a resistance, a clutching and just allow that energy to come up and allow it to pass through. Imagine never, ever, ever being able to think again. Put your head down, let the energy come up and just allow it to pass through. It's not good, it's not bad. It's just phenomena passing though. Now imagine never, ever, ever being able to think again. You've lost the ability. You might be experiencing something about HAL, the example I told you about from 2001: A Space Odyssey. CHECK AGAINST ORIG Please don't unravel me about stuff like that. Just let the energy come up, take charge, become the master and let the other energy go.

Imagine never, ever, ever being able to think again. Put your head down, see if there's any resistance or clutching and just allow the energy to come up and pass through. And more. And more. And more. And could you let go of your entire attachment to thinking? If you have a resistance to saying "yes," put your head down and allow that energy to come up and just allow it to pass through. Now notice how you feel. Are you feeling clearer and lighter, less confused? You're not feeling stupid, are you? Can you see you're getting clearer and clearer? I'm suggesting that you master your mind rather than having it master you. Could you let go of your entire attachment to thinking? See if it brings up an unwanted energy, a resistance to saying yes and just allow it to pass through. And more. And more. And even more. Keep releasing until you are clear and have no more clutching when asking the "squeezing the lemon" question. Then move on.

AVERSION TO THINKING
Stream of Consciousness:
(Just let your mind think of things about the aversion. Write it down and see what you wrote or thought as wanting approval, wanting control or wanting to be safe or secure and then release the want.)

What do I like about thinking?

_____

_____

_____

_____

What don't I like about thinking?

_____

_____

_____

1.   Imagine always thinking. You can't stop. (Let go of clutching or resist-ing the feeling it brings up in your stomach or chest. Keep releasing until there are no more feelings in your stomach or chest.)

2.   Could I let go of my entire aversion to thinking? (Keep letting go until you can say "yes" 100% with no clutching or resistance.)

Now let's continue on with our aversion to thinking. So what do you like about thinking? Does that bring up a wanting of approval, a wanting of con-trol or a wanting to be safe? Could you let go of either wanting approval, want-ing control or wanting to be safe and just let it go? And what don't you like about thinking? Does that bring up an unwanted energy or a want of approval, control or safety? And whichever it is, could you just let it go? And what else do you like about thinking? Does that bring up a wanting approval, a wanting con-trol or a wanting to be safe? And whichever it is, could you just let it go? And what don't you like about thinking? Does that bring up a want of approval, con-trol or safety? And whichever want it is, could you just let it go? Keep going back and forth until you have no more likes or dislikes and then move on.

Now let's ask the "squeezing the lemon" question about thinking. Imagine always thinking. You can't stop. You're going crazy with it. Put your head down. See if it brings up a resistance or clutching, an unwanted energy. The energy wants to leave. Just allow it to come up and allow it to pass through.

Imagine always thinking. You can't stop. It's driving you absolutely nuts. Put your head down and see if it brings up an unwanted energy, a clutching or resistance. Could you just allow it to come up and allow it to pass through. And more...and more...and even more. Imagine always thinking. You can't stop. See if it brings up a resistance, an unwanted energy. Could you just allow it to come up and allow it to pass through? And more. And more. And even more.

Imagine always thinking. You can't stop. And you're going to have to listen to this thing forever. Put your head down. See if it brings up a clutching, an unwanted energy, and just allow it to come up and allow it to pass through. And more. And more. And even more. Imagine always having to think, you can't stop. It's going to drive you nuts forever. Put your head down, allow it to come up and allow it to pass through--the energy. It's not good, it's not bad, it's just phenomenon passing through. Notice you're getting clearer and lighter. Check and see if you feel smarter or stupider. Chances are, you're feeling more and more positive, clearer and smarter. Even though your mind might have said to you "this is crazy!". So keep asking the "squeezing the lemon" question until there is no resistance in your stomach or chest area. And then move on.

Could you let go of your entire aversion to thinking?

Any resistance to saying "yes?" Put your head down and notice that there's an unwanted energy, a resistance or clutching, and allow the energy to come up and just allow it to pass through. And more. And more. And even more. Could you let go of your entire aversion to thinking? Any resistance to saying "yes?" Clutching? Just allow the energy to come up. It's not good, it's not bad. It's just phenomena passing through, so just allow that energy to be released. And more. And more. And even more. And could you let go of your entire aversion to thinking? Just allow it to come up and allow it to pass through. Keep releasing on the question until you can say "yes" 100% with no doubts or hesitation.

GETTING CLEARER AND CLEARER
Now let's do a little cleanup. And then we'll continue to get closer and closer and closer to abundance--and closer and closer to a quiet mind (if you have noticed). Now let's continue this work.

Close your eyes and see if there's an unwanted energy stirred up in your stomach or your chest area. Put your head down and put your hand on your stomach or chest area, wherever your feeling center is. And just allow that energy to come up and allow it to pass through. And more. And even more. And see if there's any more clutching or resisting in your stomach or chest area. Can you allow that energy to come up and pass through? And more. And even more. And even more. Could you let go of wanting to figure anything out? And more. And more. And even more. And could you let go of wanting know what the answers are? And more--and even more.

Now see if you can bring up some of the wanting of control--the lie that you lack control. That wanting of control. That lacking feeling. Put your head down.

Notice you have an unwanted energy. Could you just allow that energy to leave? And more. And even more. And could you let go of wanting control? That lacking control feeling? And more. And even more. And could you bring up some more of the wanting control? Just allow it to come up and allow it to pass through. And more. And even more. See if you could bring up some of the wanting approval--the lie that it lies outside yourself. That wanting, lacking feeling. Could you allow it come up? Could you allow it to pass through? And more. And more. And even more. And see if you could bring up some of the wanting to be safe, wanting to be secure--that lacking feeling. Could you allow it to come up and could you allow it to pass through? And more. And even more. Notice it gets easier. The more you practice releasing, the more you keep the "releasing muscle" open. Releasing becomes easier and easier.

ATTACHMENT TO DOING SOMETHING

Now let's look at our attachment to doing something. Now, I'm not talking about not having the ability to do something, I'm talking about being run automatically: "I gotta do this, I have to do this, I should do this, I must do this." You need to be in control rather than having to listen to this thing telling you what to do all the time.

ATTACHMENT TO DOING SOMETHING
Stream of Consciousness:
(Just let your mind think of things about the attachment. Write it down and see what you wrote or thought as wanting approval, wanting control, or wanting to be safe or secure and then release the want.)

What advantage is it to me to do something?

_____

_____

_____

_____

What disadvantage is it to me to do something?

_____

_____

_____

1.   Imagine never, ever being able to do something. (Let go of clutching or resisting the feeling it brings up in your stomach or your chest. Keep releasing

until there are no more feelings in your stomach or chest.

2. Could I let go of my entire attachment to doing something? (Keep letting go until you can say "yes" 100% with no clutching or resistance.)

So let's take a look at the attachment to doing something. So what advantage is it to you to do something? Does that bring up a feeling of wanting approval, control or safety? And could you let go of wanting approval, control or safety?

Now what disadvantage is to for you to do something? Does that bring up a feeling of wanting approval, wanting control or wanting to be safe? And could you let go of any or all of these feelings? Now what advantage is it to you to do something? Does that bring up a wanting of approval, control or safety? And could you let go of such wanting? And what disadvantage is it for you to do something? Does that bring up a wanting of approval, control or safety? Now could you let go of wanting approval, control or being safe? And what is another advantage of doing something? Does that bring up a feeling of wanting approval, control or safety? And could you let go of either wanting approval, control or being safe and secure? And what is another advantage of doing something? Could you see that as wanting approval, wanting control or wanting to be safe? And could you let it go? And more. And more.

And what's another advantage of doing something? Does that bring up a feeling of wanting approval, wanting control or wanting to be safe? And could you let go of either wanting approval, wanting control or wanting to be safe? And what's another disadvantage of doing something? Does that bring up a feeling of wanting approval, control or safety? And could you let go of either wanting approval, wanting control or wanting to be safe? Keep releasing until you have no more advantages or disadvantages coming up. Then move on.

Now we're going to ask the "squeezing the lemon" question. Again, this is designed to bring up whatever resistance you have--whatever energy is stored in your stomach or your chest area--and allow it to come up and let it go. So imagine never, ever, ever being able to do something again. You can't do it if you want to. Put your head down and allow that energy to come up and let go of resisting it. And more. And more. And even more. Imagine never, ever, ever being able to do something again. You couldn't do it even if you wanted to. And just allow that energy to come up and allow it to pass through. And more. And more. And even more. Imagine never, ever, ever being able to do something again. Allow that energy to come up and just allow it to pass through. And more. And more. And even more. Imagine never, ever, ever being able to do something again. You couldn't do it even if you wanted to. Put your head down, see if there's any unwanted energy, and just allow it to come up and allow it to pass through. And more. And more. And even more. And could you let go of your entire attachment to doing something? If there's any resistance to saying yes, put your head down and just allow that energy to come up and allow it to pass through. Keep releasing on the "squeezing the lemon" question until you have no more charge on the question.

Remember, we're going for the ability to freely do something or not do something. To eliminate that compulsion, the "I have to do this" or "I have to do that" scenario. That's all we're doing. Could you let go of your entire attachment to doing something? If there's any resistance to saying yes, just allow it to pass through. Remember, you want to be able to be free to do it or not do it. Again, why not be in control of your emotions instead of your emotions controlling you? So could you let go some more? Keep releasing until you can answer yes 100% to this question--then move on.

AVERSION TO DOING SOMETHING
Stream of Consciousness:
(Just let your mind think of things about the aversion. Write it down and see what you wrote or thought of as wanting approval, wanting control or wanting to be safe or secure and then release the want.)

What do I like about doing something?

_____

_____

_____

_____

What don't I like about doing something?

_____

_____

_____

_____

1.   Imagine always having to do something; you can't stop. (Keep releasing until there are no more feelings in your stomach or chest.)
2.   Could I let go of my entire aversion to doing something? (Keep letting go until you can say "yes" 100% with no clutching or resistance.)
And now let's look at the aversion to doing something. What do you like about doing something? Does that bring up a wanting of approval, a wanting of

control or a wanting to be safe? Could you let go of either wanting approval, wanting control or wanting to be safe? Now what don't you like about doing something? Does that bring up a wanting of approval, control or safety? And whatever it is, could you let go of either wanting approval, control or safety? Now what do you like about something? Another one. Can you see that as wanting approval, wanting control or wanting to be safe? And could you let go of any or all of those wants? And what don't you like about doing something? Could you see this as wanting approval, wanting control or wanting to be safe? And could you let go of whatever got stirred up? And what's one more "What do I like about doing something?" Does that bring up a wanting of approval, control or safety? And could you let any or all of those wants go? And what don't you like about doing something? Does that bring up a wanting of approval, a wanting of control or wanting of safety and security? And whichever want it brings up, could you now let it go? And more. And even more. Keep releasing until you have no more advantages or disadvantages. Then move on.

And now let's ask the "squeezing the lemon" question: Imagine always having to do something. You can't stop. If that brings up a clutching, a resistance, put your head down. Allow that energy to come up and allow it to leave. And more. And more. Imagine always having to do something. You can't stop, you're gonna have to do it forever. Allow that energy to come up and just let go of resisting it, and allow it to pass through. It's not good, it's not bad, it's just phenomena passing through. And more. Imagine always having to do something. You can't stop. Put your head down, allow that energy to come up. Let go of rejecting, resisting, clutching. Just allow it to pass through. And more. And more. Keep releasing until you have no more clutching from asking yourself this question. Then move on.

And could you let go of your entire aversion to doing something? Any resistance to saying yes? Put your head down, allow that energy to come up and allow it to just pass through. And could you let go of your entire aversion to doing something? Any energy there? Just allow it to come up and allow it to pass through. And could you let go of your entire aversion to doing something? And more. And even more. Keep releasing until you can say "yes" to this question 100%.

You might want to write down some insights that you have noticed when doing this exercise. The exercises are designed to help you discriminate on your attachments and aversions. They are designed to allow yourself to give up the automatic reactions and have a clear understanding of why we're doing things from an automatic standpoint of view.

PONDER: WORRYING, THINKING, DOING SOMETHING
(Why We Do It Automatically)

Here's why I suggest you do the "worrying, thinking, doing something" exercises. By doing these exercises, it allows you to call up the subconscious mind, look at it, and then release what you don't want.

The habit of worrying is something that plagues us all, but we seem to do it a lot. One day, when I was into worrying, I sat down and did an attachment to worrying and an aversion to worrying. The word "thinking" kept coming up in the releasing exercise, so I sat down and did an attachment to thinking and an aversion to thinking. To my amazement, I noticed that in order to "worry," I had to "think." In order to "think," I had to "worry." That "worrying" went hand in hand with "thinking." I never saw that in myself that way. Then the words "doing something" kept coming up, so I sat down and did an attachment to doing something and an aversion to doing something. I then discovered that every time I was worrying and thinking, I always HAD to do something. Then I noticed that I was motivating myself with negativity to do something about the disturbing or scary situation. I decided that I no longer wanted to motivate myself with negativity, so I sat down and I wrote the following goal, which I have been using successfully for years:

"I allow myself to do absolutely nothing (except release) and have a wonderful abundant life with ease."

I then discovered that the most powerful action I could take was releasing. Everything started to happen for me without me moving my muscles--the "butt" system started to work big time, and I started to know how the mind really worked. Try it. You'll like it.

CHAPTER EIGHTEEN

HOW TO ACHIEVE GOALS BY RELEASING

"If you know where you're going,
it will make the journey easier."
--Lester Levenson

According to Lester, every mind uses the very same unlimited intelligence. Everyone uses it as much as he believes he can use it to fulfill his desires. When he learns that his mental limitations are self-imposed, he lets go of them. Then his intelligence (I.Q.) can be raised to the degree of no limitation. As Lester said, "Never think of things as coming in the future, as the mind will keep it in the future. See it, feel it, taste it, possess it as yours now. Do not see it in its 'will-be-ness.'"

In this chapter, we're going to work on goals. It's very important to understand how to use goals and frame them properly to allow yourself to have everything you want in life. If you don't know where you're going, you can't get there. The use of goals will allow you to be clear about what you're doing and how to accomplish the goal you go for. So we're going to practice on how to phrase goals. We're going to show you how to use goals and how to accomplish them.

The first thing I would like you to do is to take a few minutes to think about some goals that you really would like to accomplish. We have included some suggested goals in the book and you might look them over so that you might get clearer about which ones to work on. For example, one goal might be to "allow myself to release naturally with ease." This would be a goal on releasing. Another goal might be to "allow myself to experience my full abundance and wealth every day." Also, you might consider: "allow myself to have an abundant cash flow with ease" or "allow myself to be the ideal weight for my body." You can work on any one goal you want to focus upon or take on as many as you'd like. So take a few minutes and begin to think about a goal.

Now, please read the "Wording a Goal statement" structure below and move on to the next step.

WORDING A GOAL STATEMENT
1. **Phrase it in the NOW**, as thoughit is already achieved. Phrasing it as a future event tends to keep it always out of reach--in the future.
2. **Phrase the goal positively**, without any negatives. Put in what you want, not

what you don't want. Your goal statement should reflect the end result that you want to achieve. Therefore, be sure you do not include in your statement those things you want to get rid of. Keeping it in your mind tends to create it.

3.   **It should feel real, realistic and right to you**. In other words, it should feel "possible," with a sense of "I can have it."

4.   **Include yourself** in the statement in relationship to the goal.

5.   **Be precise and concise.** Use as few words as possible while being sure to make it a complete statement of what you want. Choose the exact words that convey a specific meaning to you.

6.   **Be specific, but not limiting.** Don't limit the results by including limiting specifics. Leave things open as much as possible to allow for results being upgraded from what you initially project.

7.   **Word it to facilitate your letting go**.

8.   **Eliminate the word "want."**

9.   **State the goal or end result** and not the means (how you're planning to get it). These action possibilities would more appropriately go on your goal "to do" list.

10. **Focus on one goal per statement.** Don't diffuse your energy by creating multiple goals in a goal statement.

And now let's talk about wording your goal. Let's review the procedure again. First, phrase it in the now, as though it is already achieved. Phrasing it in the future tends to keep it out of reach--always in the future.

Secondly, phrase the goal positively, without any negatives. Put in what you want, not what you don't want. For example, I wouldn't put in "I allow myself to get rid of all my problems." If you worked on that goal, you'd be holding in mind problems--therefore perpetuating them. You might word it to say, "I allow my life to be easier" instead, or "I allow my life to be easy and effortless."

Your goal should reflect the end result that you want to achieve. Therefore, be sure not to include your statement those things you want to get rid of. Keeping it in mind tends to create it. So, hold in mind what you want--not what you don't want. It's very important.

The goal should be realistic and feel right to you. You should have a tingle, like "Yeah! This is what I want!" There should be a sense of possibility, as in "I can have it!" Don't make it a long goal. Don't have it go on and on, such as "I allow myself to have enough money to have a beautiful house and have a beautiful wife and be happy and..." . You know. Just keep it short. Include yourself in the statement in relationship to the goal: "I allow myself to _____". Make the statement precise and concise. Use as few words as possible and try to be as exacting as possible.

Be specific, but not limiting. Don't limit a result by including limitations.

Leave things open as much as possible to allow results to develop into something more than you initially projected. For example, "I allow myself to have one hundred dollars this week with ease." A better way of putting it might be, "I allow myself to have a hundred dollars or more with ease." This way, you're not limiting yourself.

Word your goal to facilitate your letting go. Eliminate the word "want" in it. Focus on one goal per statement. Let's move further. There are again some samples for you to use. You can choose a number of them or do one at a time. Releasing on goals is a most powerful way of allowing yourself to have goals in life. Use the following charts to aid you in this process.

SAMPLE GOAL STATEMENTS
Job/Career/Financial
I decide to experience my full abundance and wealth every day.
I allow myself to perform effectively and successfully at work.
I allow myself to release with ease throughout my workday.
I allow myself to easily have and enjoy the best job for me at this time in my life.
I allow myself to easily find and develop a career which will greatly utilize my creative abilities (and/or skills) and provide abundant financial rewards.
I allow myself to have an abundant cash flow of $_____ with ease.
I allow myself to have _____ dollars or more this week by releasing only.

Relationship/Communication
I allow my relationship with _____ to be joyful, loving and supportive.
I allow myself to easily and effectively communicate with _____.
I allow my situation with _____ to be resolved with fairness and mutuality for all concerned.
I allow myself to love and accept (or forgive) myself (or _____) no matter what.
I allow myself to love _____ .

Diet
I allow myself to easily achieve and maintain my ideal body weight.
I allow myself to enjoy eating foods that keep my body slender, healthy and fit.

General Health
I allow myself to release naturally and with ease.
I allow myself to sleep well and awake refreshed, well-rested at _____a.m.
I effortlessly allow myself to live at optimum health and well-being.
I allow myself to enjoy being a nonsmoker.
I allow myself to lovingly support _____ in their growth (and freedom).
I allow _____ to have what they want for themselves.

Please note: Use the foregoing as a basis for creating your own individual goal statements. Simply adjust the final wording to reflect your particular situation.

Goal Chart

Goals I Would Like to Achieve

Goal:

_____

_____

_____

_____

What is my NOW feeling about my goal?   Let go?   Feel good?

_____

_____

_____

_____

_____

_____

_____

_____

_____

_____

_____

_____

So word a goal. Write it down. Make it as positive as possible--don't place negative in the goals.

Now have a goal in mind that you want to work on and just follow my words. Look at the goal, see if it brings up a thought or feeling--whatever it is. And could you see that as either a wanting of approval, a wanting of control or a wanting to be safe and secure? And whichever want it brings up, could you let go of it?

Now take a look at the goal again and see what thought or feeling it conjures up. Whichever it is, write it down. Could you see that as either wanting approval, control or safety? And could you let go of these wants? Take a look at the goal again. See what thought it conjures up. Does that stir up a wanting of approval, control or safety? And could you let go of any or all of these wants?

Now look at the goal again. See if it's more possible or less possible to attain the goal. If you've been releasing, you're going to see and find that it's more possible. So what's the next thought or feeling that gets conjured up as you look at the goal? Does that bring up a wanting of approval, control or safety? And could you let go of either wanting approval, control or safety? Take a look at the goal again. What's the next feeling or thought it conjures up? Could you see that as either wanting approval, control or safety and security? And could you let go of wanting approval, control or safety and security?

And now look at the goal again. Does it conjure up a thought or a feeling? And whichever feeling it conjures up, could you see that as either wanting approval, control or safety? And could you let go of either wanting approval, control or safety? And now look at the goal again. See what it conjures up in your mind. Does that equate to a wanting of approval, control or safety? Whichever feeling gets stirred up, could you let it go?

Now you keep releasing on your goal until the feeling is "I have it. It's mine right now." And you keep following the same procedure, you keep releasing on it until it falls into your lap--until you actually have it in your hand. (Now THINK you have it, actually HAVE it in your hand.) If you keep working on a goal and it's exactly what you really want, it will fall in your lap shortly.

What to do if you don't achieve the goal
If you work on a goal for more than two weeks and it doesn't happen, I recommend that you do advantages and disadvantages of having that goal. You might discover that subconsciously you don't really want it and that's why it didn't fall in your lap. But if you're really, really intent on having it, it'll fall in your lap. Now, Lester felt that goals were very, very important. I recommend that you get a little notebook with blank sheets in it and write your goals daily. I have about four or five of them going all the time and I release on them daily. Then,

when I actually accomplish the goal, I circle it and I write down "I did it," so that when I flip through the pages at a later date, I see which ones I've actually accomplished and which I haven't. And if I haven't accomplished a goal, I sit down and do "Why have I created that to happen?" I do the responsibility exercise so I see it very clearly!

I ask, "Why didn't I attain the goal?" and then I let it go or I do advantages and disadvantages on having the goal. Then I release on it so I get clear about what I'm doing.

Many times, we've gone toward something, striving for it and always knowing we weren't going to win. And then we get there and we say, "I knew it." So make sure you do attachments and aversions, advantages and disadvantages on the goal, depending on how deep and strong it is. Then just release on it so you can get clear about it. I guarantee, as you keep releasing, it will fall in your lap. You must prove it to yourself. Don't believe me. Check it out and prove it to yourself. And don't just do it once. Do it repeatedly.

What Lester says about goals
"You must get to the place where you master the world because if you're not winning, if you're not a winner, you have anti-programming to being a winner. You must become a winner. You must achieve your goal so that you can bring up the anti-winning--the anti-goal--and rid yourself of it. The aversions to the world are stronger and far more subtle than the attachments. So when you go to be a winner and you go for gold, up comes your aversions and you need to be a winner just to get the garbage up and out."

Q: Did you say that your aversions are stronger than your attachments?

A: Your aversions are stronger and more subtle than your attachments. Your attachments are obvious--"I want this and I want that and I want money and I want things." So, the attachments are obvious. But the fact is, the things you don't want, you don't look at. And that develops resisting, suppression and resistance. So goals are very important on your way to becoming a winner.

It's very important to use the word "allow" when you're doing a goal because the word "allow" is a fabulous one if you can catch on to the actual experiential part. What does someone have to do to "allow" something to happen? Just let it happen. There's no wanting control there, no push, there's nothing. You just allow it to happen. Many of us have experienced ourselves allowing something to happen with ease. We call it a "zone," where everything just happens perfectly when we get out of the way and we allow it to happen. And then we try to fix it, push it and control it. It just doesn't happen that way. Just allow it to happen.

Have the words "I allow" in all your goals. "I allow myself to have an abundant cash flow." "I allow myself to be a loving being at all times." "I allow myself to experience love at all times." "I allow myself to experience abundance in every which way." And on and so forth.

You might also put in the word "ease." "I allow things to happen easily (or, by definition, with 'ease')." Many of us are putting forth effort and pushing. By putting in the word "ease," it allows things to happen easily. We are also resisting goals, so let's take a look at some of the resistance we have to achieving our goals.

Think of the goal you've been working on right now. What do you resist about doing this goal? Could you feel the resistance, the clutching? Could you let go of resistance, of clutching? And what do you resist about having this goal or accomplishing it? Put your head down and see if it brings up an unwanted energy in your stomach or your chest, a clutching or resistance. Now, just let go of resisting.

And what else do you resist about having this goal? Put your head down. See if there's an unwanted energy in your feeling center. Just allow it to pass through. Remember it's just a feeling. It's not good, it's not bad. It's just energy passing through.

And what do you resist about NOT having your goal? Put your head down. See if there's any resistance, any energy, any clutching and just allow it to pass through. And what's another thing you resist about NOT having this goal or not doing what you need to do? Just allow that energy to come up and just allow it to pass through. And what's something you resist about doing? Or something you resist about allowing it to happen? And could you let go of resisting? Could you let go of clutching? Let go of being so smart and allow it to be other than what you think it is.

That's an excellent way to neutralize a thought. Sometimes you might be standing right in front of somebody, asking them for something. Immediately your mind says, They're not going to know or they're not going to give it to me. Immediately say to yourself, Could I let go of being so smart and allow it to be other than what I think it is? And just let it go. What happens in life is whatever you think. If it's a negative thought, just immediately neutralize it by saying to yourself, Could I let go of being so smart and allow it to be other than what I think it is? You'll be amazed at what happens. The situation and the result will change. Try it. You'll like it.

CHAPTER NINETEEN

DEMONSTRATION

"A desire is a disturbance of one's natural, inherent peace and joy. Desires keep one involved in trying to satiate the desires, consequently detracting one from his constant, natural, inherent happiness. In short, desire is the enemy of happiness and the source of misery."
--Lester Levenson

LESTER LEVENSON ON DEMONSTRATION

We're now going to take a look at what Lester has to say on demonstration, in the following transcript from his "Willpower" tape:

"Whether we are aware of it or not, everyone is controlling matter all the time. Whether one wants to be a demonstrator or not, he is. It is impossible to not be a creator all the time. Everyone is creating every day. We're not aware of it because we just don't look at it. Every thought, every single thought materializes in the physical world. It's impossible to have a thought that will not materialize, except when we reverse it. If we say the opposite right after we have a thought of equal strength, we just neutralize it. But any thought not reversed or neutralized will materialize in the future, if not immediately. So this thing of demonstration that we're all trying so hard to do we're doing all the time, unaware of the fact that we are doing it. All we need to do is consciously direct it--and that we call demonstration.

Everything that everyone has in life is a demonstration. It could not come into your experience had you not had a thought of it sometime prior. If you want to know what your sum total thinkingness is, it's exactly determined by what's around you, what you have. That is your demonstration. If you like it, you may hold it. If you don't start changing your thinking, concentrate it in the direction that you really want until those thoughts become predominant--and whatever those thoughts are will materialize in the world. And when you begin to demonstrate consciously--small things--you may then realize that the only reason why they're small is because you don't dare to think big.

But the exact same rule or principle applies to demonstrating a penny that applies to demonstrating a billion dollars. The mind sets the size. Anyone who can demonstrate a dollar can demonstrate a million dollars. Become aware of the way you're demonstrating the one-dollar bill, and put six zeroes after it next time. Take on the consciousness of the million, rather than the one-dollar bill.

This relates to what I have been saying that there's no difference between the spiritual and the material when you see it, the material being just an out-projecting of our minds into what we call the universe, the world and many bodies. And when we see that it is just an out-projecting of our mind, that it's just a picture out there we have created, we can very easily change it. Instantly.

So to repeat: Everyone is demonstrating and creating during every moment that he or she is thinking. You have no choice. You are a creator so long as you have a mind and think. To get beyond creation, we must go beyond the mind--and just beyond the mind is the realm of all Knowingness, where there is no need for creation. There's a higher state than creation: It's a state of is-ness, of being-ness, sometimes called Awareness, Beingness, Consciousness. That's just behind the mind. That's beyond creation. The mind finds it very difficult to imagine what it's like beyond creation because it is involved primarily in creation--in the act of creating. It's the creating instrument of the universe and everything that happens in the world, in the universe.

If you take this thing called mind, which is only a creator, and try to imagine what it is like beyond creation, it's impossible. The mind will never know peace (quiet) because you have to go just above the mind to know peace (quiet) to know the Infinite Being that we are--to know what it's like beyond creation. The final state is beyond creation. The ultimate State is the changeless state. In creation, everything is constantly changing. Therefore, in creation, the Ultimate Truth is not there. So to demonstrate what one wants, one needs to become aware of the fact that all we need to do is to think only of the things we want, and that is all that we would get, if we would do just that.

Only think of the things you want, and that's what you'll be getting all the time, because the mind is only creative. Nice and easy, isn't it? Also, take credit for all the things you create that you don't like. Just say, "Oh, look what I did," because when you become aware that you've created things you don't like, you're still in a position of creator. If you don't like it, all you have to do is turn it upside down and you'll like it."

WHAT AM I DEMONSTRATING IN MY LIFE?

_____

_____

_____

If what you are doing in life or what is happening to you brings up a clutching or resistance in your stomach or chest, keep releasing the energy until it is completely released.

What are you demonstrating in your life? Think of one thing you're demonstrating in your life. And just let go of that energy in your feeling center. Allow it to come up and allow it to pass through, especially if you're demonstrating some negative things in your life. Think of one. Allow that energy to come up instead of pushing it down and clutching. If you're not releasing on the negativity, you're just collecting it. Welcome it up. Allow it to be there and just allow it to pass through. Put your head down. Disconnect your head and just put the tube into the energy and allow that energy to come up and out. It's not good, it's not bad--it's just phenomenon passing through. And what's something else you're demonstrating in a negative way in your life? Put your head down and notice if it brings up an unwanted energy, a clutching, a resistance, and just allow that energy to come up. It wants to leave, so just allow it to pass through.

And what's something else you're demonstrating in your life? See if just thinking about what is happening in your life results in a clutching or resistance. Just allow it to come up and allow that energy to pass through. Again, it's not good, it's not bad--it's just phenomenon coming up. And more. And more. And what's something else you're demonstrating in your life? Whatever energy it brings up, just allow it to pass through. If it's clutching or resistance, just allow it to pass through. And more. And even more. And what's something else you're demonstrating in your life? See if there's any clutching or resistance--a wanting to change it. And just allow it to come up and pass through. And more. And even more. Lester says if you don't like what you're demonstrating in life, turn it upside down (release it) and what you're demonstrating in life will turn around and change. That's what we're doing by releasing. We're just feeling the energy, letting it go and allowing it to leave.

Now think of something else you're demonstrating in your life. Maybe you have a hassle with somebody. Maybe you have a problem or argument. Maybe you're not getting along with someone. Maybe you're not having enough money. Maybe you're not in good health. All of those are demonstrations, so think of one and see if it brings up a clutching or resistance. Just allow that energy to pass through. Again, it's not bad, it's not good, it's just phenomenon passing through.

And what's something else you're demonstrating in your life? See what energy that brings up. Put your head down and allow the energy to pass through. And more. And even more.

You can release with your eyes open and you don't have to have your head down after a while, but make sure you disconnect your head. Be sure you can put your hand on your stomach or chest area, whichever is your feeling center. This is just to remind you to disconnect your head. If things become severely difficult, it's probably a good idea to put your head down and put the tube into the energy. Then just allow it to pass through.

So what else are you demonstrating in your life? Allow it to come up and just allow it to pass through. See if you're clutching. If you're not clutching, you'll notice everything is perfect--everything is OK. There's no need to change anything.

WHAT IS MY CONSCIOUSNESS ABOUT RELATIONSHIPS?

_____

_____

_____

If what you are doing in life or what is happening to you brings up a clutching or resistance in your stomach or chest, keep releasing the energy until it is completely released.

RELATIONSHIP DEMONSTRATIONS
So let's look at relationships. What are some of your concerns about relationships? What are you demonstrating in the form of relationships? Take a look. See if that brings up a resistance, a clutching or a wanting to change it; and just allow that energy to come up and pass through.

And what's another concern, another demonstration in relationships? Just allow that energy to come up and allow it to pass through. And what else is your consciousness about relationships? See what you're demonstrating. See if there's any clutching or resisting. Just allow that energy to come up and just allow it to pass through. It really wants to leave. Just allow it to pass through.

WHAT IS MY CONSCIOUSNESS ABOUT BUSINESS?

_____

_____

_____

If what you are doing in life or what is happening to you brings up a clutching or resistance in your stomach or chest, keep releasing the energy until it is completely released.

DEMONSTRATION AND BUSINESS
And now let's look at your consciousness about business. What is your consciousness about business? What are you demonstrating in business? You don't like your job? You don't have a good boss or partner? You don't like how much

money you're making? Take a look. Notice if you're clutching when you think of those things, a resisting. Put your head down. Allow that energy to come up and just allow it to erase and dissolve.

And take a look about something else you're demonstrating in business. Maybe you just don't like working but feel you have to in order to make a living. Notice if you're clutching, you want to change it. Is there a resistance? Just allow that energy to come up and just allow it to pass through.

Keep working on these questions until you're no longer bothered about what you demonstrating in your life.

CHAPTER TWENTY

PRIDE--HOW IT STOPS US
FROM HAVING ABUNDANCE

"If you could stop thinking for one moment,
you would discover what you are."
Lester Levenson

In this chapter, we're going to explore pride. We're going to move right up the Chart of Emotions from pride to courageousness. Pride, if you look at the Chart of Emotions and the Scale of Action, is a real strong "I can't." It's hidden by "I won't." People in pride often say, "I won't do it." However, we didn't ask you if you won't do it. We asked, "Can you do it?" They say, "I don't want to." Yeah, but CAN you do it? To that, they say, "I don't want to."

So pride is a HIDE. We hide things in pride and it's a very, very strong rejecting place. Pride is where all rejection happens, including our rejection of abundance. And so we're going to explore pride and allow ourselves to feel it. That way, we can let it go so we can move through it, progressing to courageousness and acceptance.

In pride, we have a feeling we are better than anyone else--that nobody else counts and everybody has to look at us and see how wonderful we are. When we make the jump to courageousness, we feel like saying, "I'm terrific, you're terrific; we'll all move together." There's no contest. The contest stops and so does the conflict and fight to better than the next person. We are very rejecting in pride and we need to explore that and release it, dumping it all so we can move up the Chart of Emotions toward courageousness, acceptance and peace.

So let's read pride from the Scale of Action. Lester's definition of pride: "Pride is the wish to maintain the status quo, unwilling to change or move. Therefore, the wish to stop others from movement as they might pass us up." It's a contest--"I have to be better than everybody. If you try to move past me, I'm going to push you down."

COURAGEOUSNESS--WHAT THAT LOOKS LIKE
Courageousness is the willingness to move out without fear or hesitation--to do, to correct, to change--whatever is needed. It's the willingness to let go and move on.

Ask the releasing questions of: "Would you let it go? Could you let it go? When?" These are courageous questions. They're not prideful questions, they're courageous ones. Would you let it go? Could you let it go? When? The questions move you up to courageousness, giving you back your power. You recognize it's your feelings. Since they're your feelings, you can let them go if you choose to. Doing this continuously moves you closer to acceptance and peace. Therefore, you move toward the imperturbable person you are.

The more you move up on the chart (if you haven't noticed), the quieter you get, the more powerful you get, the more capable you are, the more positive you are. As we've been letting go of these limiting feelings, we are moving up the chart. We've been letting go of this energy and allowing it to pass through. You might take a few minutes and turn to the Chart of Emotions. Check to see where on the chart you were when you started to do the work in this book. Where are you right now on the Chart of Emotions?

Notice that you moved up. Most of us bounce around from different places on the Chart of Emotions, but we all have a home base we can generally hang out in. You will notice that the more you have been releasing these limitations called feelings, the more you've moved up the chart.

Now we're going to take a look at pride in a more in-depth way. In Chapter Eight, there's a description of pride. Let's look at pride again.

The way you feel in pride is: above it all, aloof, arrogant, better than, complacent, conceited, condescending, contemptuous, cool, disdain, haughty, holier-than-thou, icy, irreverent, judgmental, pious, righteous, rigid, smug, special, superior, uncompromising, unfeeling, vain.

And the way you think when you're in pride includes:
How dare you?
I knew that.
I know everything.
I know.
I won't associate with THOSE kind of people.
I'll look like I'm agreeing and I'll do it my way.
I'm better than all of them.
I'm better than you.
I'm in a better place than all of you.
I'm not like them.
I'm the only one who can do it right.
I'm the only one who can get it done.
I'm the savior.
I'm the hero.
I'm too busy with important matters to have time for you.
It's your fault.
Maybe I'll do it and maybe I won't.

My way is the only way.
What do they know?
What's wrong with you?
Who do they think they are?
Who do you think you are?
Why is everyone so incompetent?
You don't belong.
You need me to get it done.

The way you act when being prideful is: aloof, arrogant, bigoted, blaming others, boastful, bored, closed, complacent, conceited, detached, disrespectful, distant, dogmatic, egotistical, false humility, gloating, hypocritical, indifferent, know-it-all, narrow-minded, never wrong, opinionated, patronizing, pompous, putting others down, remote, sabotaged, sanctimonious, self-absorbed, self-centered, self-important, snobbish, spoiled, stoic, stubborn, stuck up, talking against others, unforgiving, impenetrable, unreadable, unyielding, withdrawn.

Take a look at somebody you know in your life that's in pride a lot and see if you're rejecting, resisting or clutching in reaction to how they act. And just allow that energy to come up and allow it to pass through. And think about a time when you acted in pride--when you really, really thought you were the cat's meow--and you got smashed for it. See if there's any resistance, any rejection, any clutching. Just allow that energy to come up and allow it to pass through.

LETTING GO OF PRIDE ALLOWS US TO MOVE UP TO CAP

One must be OK with any energy. Therefore, we need to move through the energy and push through it, allowing the flow of abundance to continue. Now, when we don't like somebody in pride, guess what? We're in pride and we don't really know it. We're judging them. We're making them wrong and we're actually rejecting them. We end up feeling rejected, BUT IT'S NOT POSSIBLE TO FEEL REJECTED IF YOU AREN'T THE REJECTOR. Just take a check and see. It's not possible to feel rejected if you aren't clutching or resisting. Next time you feel rejected, put your head down, notice if there's an unwanted energy in your stomach or chest. Allow it to come up and allow it to pass through.

MOVING FROM A VICTIM PLACE TO A CAUSAL PLACE

Think about the last time you felt rejected. Put your head down and see if you have an unwanted energy in your stomach or chest area. Just allow it to come up and allow it to pass through. Think about the last time you rejected someone. You judged them, you put them down. Could that be pride? Could you put your head down and notice there's an unwanted energy there? Could you allow it to come up and pass through? And think about somebody who's really in pride. See if that brings up any resistance in your feeling center--somebody acting like that, walking around like that. See if you're rejecting, resisting them inside your feeling center. Could you allow your energy to come up and just allow it to pass through?

Think about the last time somebody was teasing you or you were teasing them. Could that be pride? It looks playful, but still there's a lot of negative energy there. Take a check. Just allow that energy to come up. Let go of resisting it. It's wanting to get the other person, wanting to show the other person. Can't you see it? Can't you feel it? Feel that pride. Allow it to come up and allow it to pass through.

COURAGEOUSNESS
Let's take a look at courageousness. It's not a holding back place, it's a giving place. Courageousness is the willingness to move out without fear or hesitation. To do. To correct. To change whatever is needed. The willingness to let go and move on. And the feelings associated with courageousness are: alert, alive, assured, aware, centered, cheerful, clear, confident, cooperative, delighted, eager, energetic, exhilarated, focused, grounded, full of gusto, happy, heartiness, hopeful, independent, invincible, loving, lucid, nonresistant, open, optimistic, passionate, purposeful, receptive, resilient, safe, secure, stable, willing, zealous and zestful.

And the way you think when you're in courageousness: I can, I can get it done. I can listen. I can respond appropriately. I do what is needed and it works. I know we can. I'll do what it takes to make it work. I'm willing. I'm willing to take risks. It can be easy and effortless. It is as easy as it is hard. It's possible. Let's work together. We can do it. We'll find a way. Yes!

In pride, you're actually feeling: I'm the greatest and don't you dare do anything to stop me. Everybody look at me. In courageousness: We're terrific. I'm terrific, you're terrific, we'll all be terrific and we'll help each other.

That's a big shift--a big difference. And the way you act is: able, aboveboard, adaptive, adventurous, bold, brave, candid, collaborative, committed, compassionate, competent, cooperative, creative, daring, decisive, dedicated, dynamic, enjoyably, exploratory, flexible, focused, forthright, gallant, generous, giving, full of goodness, gratified, honestly, humorous, initiative, inquiringly, insightful, full of integrity, inventive, motivated, partnering, perceptive, persevering, persistent, playful, pleasurably, resourceful, risk-taking, robust, self-sufficient, sharp, solution-focused, spontaneous, strong, supportive, tireless, unpretentious, valiant and vigorous.

So take a look at the times when you've been in courageousness. See what it looks like. It's a big shift from pride, which is "I'm terrific and don't try to be better than me," to courageousness, which is "I'm terrific, you're terrific...we'll help each other." It's an attitude swing, it's an energy shift, and it's a moving closer and closer to acceptance and peace.

LETTING GO OF PRIDE AND MOVING UP

Now let's take a look at "Releaing the Pride". The following exercise is designed to allow you to let go of your pride and move up into beingness faster.

Pride is an emotion that gets us stuck because often we want to hold on to it and protect it. Pride is sometimes a sense of having done it and not being sure if we can do it again. Therefore, we hold on to what we've done and try to get acknowledgment for it instead of just moving on to our next accomplishment. It's also sometimes a subtle sense of being better than others.

Pride is a blind spot for most of us. We often get stuck in pride and don't know it. Doing this exercise will uncover your pride for yourself and let it go. What I want you to do is just follow along and see what happens.

RELEASING PRIDE

1. Ask yourself "What am I proud of?" Make a list and release the wants associated with each item. Do one at a time.
2. Ask yourself, "Could I let go of holding on to the pride?"
3. Things that people are often proud about, that we are not consciously aware of:
*being stubborn
*being able to drive others crazy by acting negatively
*being a woman or being a man
*being smart
*being proud of certain things you do in life
*being a smart ass or a brat...
You get the idea!

So, think about something you're proud about. Whatever it is--being a smart ass, being stubborn, being smarter than most people, being able to drive people crazy--whatever it is you're proud of. Write it down. I want you to dig as deep as you can. Write down and notice the things that you are proud about that you hide from yourself and don't want even yourself--and definitely others --to know. So think of one thing that you're proud of. Could you see that as either wanting approval, wanting control or wanting safety and security? And could you let go of either wanting approval, control or safety and security? And think of something else you're proud of. Whichever want it stirs up, could you just let it go?

Now think of something else you're proud of. Remember, pride is a holding-on feeling. So, could you even let go of pride of your son or daughter for a past accomplishment? It's OK to be proud of your son or daughter, but sometimes we hold on to the pride so we can't move forward. Let go and move up. Just let go of the pride and see if it gets any better. Don't just stay stuck. So see what else you're proud of. Could you let that go? And more. And even more. And think of something else you're proud of. Dig as deep as you can. And could you let that go? Could you let go of being proud of that? And more. And more. And I'm not saying it's bad to proud, I'm just saying it's OK to feel it, but then move on. Move up to courageousness, acceptance and peace. Don't just stay stuck in pride. And more. And more.

Now think of something else you're proud of but you don't want anybody else to know. Could you allow that pride to come up? And just allow it to pass through. And more. And even more. And even more. And think of something else you're proud of. Could you let go of being proud of that? It's just an energy. Put your head down, allow the energy to come up and allow it to pass through so you can move up to courageousness and peace. Don't just hold on, let it go. And see what else you've brought up. Could that be wanting approval, control or safety? Whichever want it is, could you just allow it to pass through?

Think of something else you're proud of. Put your head down and notice there's a clutching, an energy there. And just allow it to come up and allow it to pass through. And think of something else you're proud of and allow that energy to come up and pass through. Keep releasing all of your price and then continue.

JUDGMENTS

In this section, we're going to explore judgment. So right now let's ask some more questions. Who or what are you judging? Put your head down, notice there's a clutching, an energy there. And could you let go of judging? And more. And more. Think of somebody you're judging. It could be yourself. It could be somebody else. Notice it's uncomfortable. Put your head down and just allow that energy to come up. Don't release for them, release for you, and allow that energy to leave. And more. And even more. Think of something else you're judging. And just allow that energy to come up and let go of judging it, just allow it to pass through. And think of something or somebody you have a judgment about. Could you allow that energy to come up in your stomach or your chest and just allow it to pass through. And more. And more.

Are you judging yourself for judging yourself or for judging other people? Could you let go of judging yourself? And more. And more. And more. Are you judging somebody for being in pride? Are you proud of being proud? Or proud of being judgmental? Whichever energy it stirs up, could you just allow it to pass through? And more. And more. And even more. And think of somebody else or something else you're judging. And could you let it go? And more. And more. And more. Keep releasing in the judging until you are clear before moving on. Now think of something you're guilty about. It's another form of judgment. Could you allow that energy to come up, let go of resisting it, let go of clutching and just allow it to pass through? And more. And more. And more. It's just a habit.

GUILT

Think of something you're guilty about. Just allow that energy to come up. Put your head down, allow it to come up and allow it to pass through. And more. And even more. And think of something you did in the past that you feel guilty about. Put your head down. It's silly to feel guilty about it. You're just hurting yourself and you're just judging yourself (if you've ever noticed). And that is also pride. Can you allow that energy to come up and allow it to pass through? And more. And even more. Think of someone who judges you or judges other people. Are you judging them back for doing that? Put your head down and notice there's an energy there and just allow it to pass through. And more. And even more.

And think of something else you're guilty about, something you're guilty for doing. Just allow that energy to come up and allow it to pass through. Keep releasing until the guilt is gone, then move on.

SEPARATION

All right, let's take a look at separation. Who or what do you want to be separate from? Whatever answer you've got, could you put your head down and allow the energy to come up and allow it to pass through? Notice there's a clutching going on, a resistance, and just allow it to pass through. And more. And even more. Who or what do you want to be separate from? Think of some feeling you want to be separate from. Put your head down. Notice there's a resistance there and just allow it to pass through. And more. And more. Think of something else you want to be separate from. And outrageous person, an annoying person. Put your head down and notice that there's judging going on. And it's uncomfortable. Allow that energy to come up and allow it to just pass through. And more. And even more. Do you want to be separate from your feelings? Keep releasing on things you want to be separate from until you're clear on it before moving on.

REJECTING

Now think of somebody you're rejecting. Could you let go of rejecting them? And more. And more. And maybe you're rejecting yourself--a habit or something you do that you don't like. Put your head down and allow that energy to come up and just allow it to pass through. And more. And even more. Now think of somebody you're rejecting. Just allow that energy to come up and allow it to pass through. And more. And even more. And think of somebody that is rejecting you. Could you allow that energy to come up and allow it to pass through? And more. And more.

Now think of somebody you're resisting or something that you're resisting. Maybe it's a feeling like apathy, grief, fear, lust, anger, pride or even CAP. Just allow that energy to come up. Put your head down, just allow it to pass through. And more. And more. And more. It's only because you're resisting that you feel a push and feel uncomfortable. Let go of resisting. And more. And more.

And think of somebody or something you're resisting. Could you be resisting abundance or having an easy life? Could you be resisting having lots of money or having a loving person in your life? Could you let go of resisting those things? And more. And even more. And even more. And again, anytime you wish, you can stop and do more work on each of these subjects. I highly recommend it.

JEALOUSY

So who or what brings up feelings of jealousy for you? Think of somebody you're jealous of or something that you're jealous about. Just allow that energy to come up. Notice if you're clutching, if there's a resistance. Just allow that energy to pass through. And more. And more. Think of somebody you're jealous of. See if there's a clutching, a resistance and just allow that energy to pass through. And think of somebody you're in contest with. See if they're jealous of you and whether you're rejecting them or not. Could you let go of rejecting them? And more. And more. And could you let go of trying to separate yourself from them? And more--and even more.

BEING BETTER THAN OTHERS

And think of somebody you think you are better than--one person whom you think you're better than. Could you allow that person to be equal to you? Let go of clutching and just release it. Think of somebody you think you are better than. Could you allow that person to be equal to you? And now just let it go. And think of somebody else you think you're better than--one person you think you are better than. Could you allow that person to be equal to you? Let go of clutching and release it. Think of somebody else you think you're better than. Could you allow that person to be equal to you? And just let it go.

Now you may want to take the time at this point and continue on with a number of people in your life and let go of this stuff.

INSECURITY

Now, who do you think is better than you? Think of one person that you think is better than you. Can you allow yourself to be equal to them? Could you allow yourself to be equal to them? Notice if there's any clutching. Just let it go. Now who do you think is better than you? Think of one person that you think is better than you. Could you allow yourself to be equal to them? Notice if there's any clutching, release on it, and then let it go! You may want to stop here and continue on with some other people before moving forward.

Now one more: Think of somebody you think is better than you. This person might be more accomplished, have more money, might be better looking or more comfortable in life. Notice you're clutching, judging either yourself or them, and just allow that energy to leave and pass through.

PERSONALITY

And now let's take a look at our persona, our personality. A better name for it may be "poison"-ality if you are in pride. Take one personality flaw that you have or personality trait that you have and see if it's a wanting of approval, control or safety. And could you let go of either wanting control, wanting approval or wanting safety and security? It might be that you're gentle at times. Could you see that as either wanting approval, control or safety? And could you let that go? It could be that you're tough at times--even mean. You get the idea.

Pick one personality trait that you have and see if it's a wanting of approval, control or safety. And could you let go of either wanting approval, control or safety? Pick another personality trait that you have and see if it's a wanting of approval, control or safety. And could you let go of either wanting approval, control or safety? Pick one personality trait that you have and see if it's a wanting of approval, control or safety. And could you let go of either wanting approval, control or safety? At this point, you might want to continue letting go of your personality traits, your persona--letting it go so you're not stuck in pride and you can move on and allow the flow of abundance to continue.

Doing this work is very important in order to move into abundance. So go back and do more until it is all cleared up before moving on.

ATTACHMENT AND AVERSION TO PRIDE

In this part, we're going to continue looking at pride and our resistance to it. We're going to look at resistance.

And let's do an attachments and aversions session with pride. So what do you like about pride? Does that bring up a wanting of approval, control or safety and security? And whichever want it brings up, could you let it go? And what disadvantage is it for you to be in pride? Does that bring up a wanting of approval, control or safety? And whichever want it stirs up, could you let it go? Could you even let go of wanting to be separate? And what's another advantage of you being in pride? Does that bring up a wanting of approval, control or safety or wanting to be separate? And whichever want it brings up, could you just let it go? And what's another disadvantage of you being in pride or having pride? Does that bring up a wanting of approval, control, safety or separation? And whichever want it is, could you just let it go? And what's another advantage to being in pride? Does that bring up a wanting of approval, control, safety or separation? And whichever want it is, could you just let it go? And what's a disadvantage of being in pride or having pride? Does that bring up a wanting of approval, control, safety or separation? And whichever want it is, could you let it go? Could you just let it go?

Now let's ask the "squeezing the lemon" question with regard to pride. Imagine never, ever, ever being able to have pride again. If that brings up an unwanted energy in your stomach or chest--a rejection, a clutching or resistance--could you just let it go? And more. And even more. Imagine never, ever, ever being able to have pride again. You lost the ability. Notice if it brings up an unwanted energy in your stomach or chest area, a resistance, a clutching--allow it come up and allow it to pass through. And more. And even more. And could you let go of your entire attachment to pride? Any resistance to saying "yes," just allow that energy to come up and allow it to pass through. Remember that we are moving up towards imperturbability, courageousness, acceptance and peace. And each time we let go, we're moving up. And pride is a big stuck place, a resistant place. And could you let go of your entire attachment to pride? Could you just allow that energy to pass through? Any resistance to saying "yes?" Just let it go. And more. And even more.

AVERSION TO PRIDE
And now let's do the aversion to pride. What do you like about pride? Does that bring up a wanting of approval, control, safety or separation? And could you let go of these wants? And what do you dislike about pride? Does that bring up a wanting of approval, control, safety or separation? And whichever want it is, could you just allow it to pass through? And what do you like about pride? Does that bring up a wanting of approval, control, safety or separation? And whichever want it stirs up, could you just let it go? Just allow it to pass through. It's not good, it's not bad, it's just phenomenon passing through. And what don't you like about pride? Does that bring up a wanting of approval, control, safety or separation? And whichever one it stirs up, could you just let it go?

And now let's ask the "squeezing the lemon" question with regard to pride. Imagine always being in pride all the time. Wherever you go, you can't stop. See if it brings up a clutching, a resistance, and just allow the energy to come up and allow it to pass through. And more. And even more. Imagine always being in pride. You're going to walk around in pride all the time. You can't stop, and people are going to pop you for it. See if that brings up an unwanted energy and just allow it to come up and pass through. And more. And more. Imagine always being in pride. All the time. And you're going to be surrounded by other people in pride and you can't stop. Just notice if it brings up an unwanted energy, a clutching, a resistance, and just allow it to pass through. And more. And more. Could you let go of your entire aversion to pride? If there's any resistance to saying "yes," let go of resisting, let go of clutching, and just allow that energy to pass through. And more. And more. Remember it's not good, it's not bad--it's just phenomenon passing through. And more. And even more.

ATTACHMENT AND AVERSION TO RESISTANCE

Now let's take a look at our attachment and aversion to resistance. Resistance really stops us from going all the way, to just letting go and going all the way to imperturbability and having abundance. It's all resistance. So let's take a look at it. What advantage is it for you to resist? Does that bring up a wanting of approval, control or safety? And could you let go of either wanting approval, control or safety? And what disadvantage is it for you to resist? Does that bring up a wanting of approval, control or safety? And could you let go of those wants? What advantage is it for you to resist? Does that bring up a wanting of approval, control or safety? And could you let go of either wanting approval, control or safety? And what disadvantage is it for you to resist? Does that bring up a wanting of approval, control or safety? And could you let go of those wants? And what's another advantage of you to resist? Does that bring up a wanting of approval, control or safety? And could you let go of either one of those wants? And what's another disadvantage of you to resist? Does it bring up a wanting of approval, control, safety or separation? And could you let go of any or all of these wants?

Now one more: What advantage is it to you to resist? Does that bring up a wanting of approval, control, safety or separation? And could you let go of any or all of these wants? And what disadvantage is it to you to resist? Does that bring up a wanting of approval, control, safety or separation? And whichever want it stirs up, could you let that go?

And now let's ask the "squeezing the lemon" question. Imagine never, ever being able to resist again. You can't do it if you wanted to. Put your head down and see if that brings up an unwanted energy. Could you let go of that resisting energy? Just allow it to come up and allow it to pass through. Imagine never, ever, ever being able to resist again. You can't do it. Allow that energy to come up--that resistance in your stomach or your chest area--and allow it to pass through. You're not on automatic. You can do it when you decide to do it. Just let the energy pass through. Imagine never, ever being able to resist again. You lost the ability. If that brings up a clutching, an uncomfortable feeling, then just allow that energy to pass through.

And could you let go of your entire attachment to resistance? If you're having difficulty saying "yes," put your head down and notice if there's a resistance, a clutching, and just allow that energy to come up and pass through.

And could you let go of your entire attachment to resistance? Just allow that energy to come up. Anything stopping you from saying "yes?" Let it come up and allow it to pass through.

AVERSION TO RESISTANCE

And now let's do the aversion to resistance. What do you like about resistance? Does that bring up a wanting of approval, control, safety or separation? And could you let go of any or all of these wants? And more. And more. And what don't you like about resistance? Does that bring up a wanting of approval, control, safety or separation? Now what do you like about resistance? Does that bring up a wanting of approval, control, safety or separation? And could you let go of these wants? And what don't you like about resistance? Does that bring up a wanting of approval, control, safety or separation? And could you let go of these wants? And, again, what do you like about resistance? Does that bring up a wanting of approval, control, safety or separation? And could you let go of any or all of these wants?

Now let's ask the "squeezing the lemon" question. Imagine always resisting--all the time. You can't stop. Put your head down and see if that brings up an unwanted energy. Is there a clutching, a resistance? And could you just let go of that energy? Just allow it to come up. Just allow it to leave. It's not good, it's not bad, it's just passing through. Imagine always resisting, all the time. You can't stop. See if that brings up an unwanted energy and just allow it to come up and allow it to pass through.

One more time: Imagine always resisting all the time. You can't stop. And you're surrounded by people who are resisting. See if that brings up a clutching. Put your head down. Notice the unwanted energy in your stomach or chest. Allow it to come up and allow it to pass through. And could you let go of your entire aversion to resisting? Could you let go of your entire aversion to resistance? Anything stopping you from saying "yes?" Just put your head down, see if there's a clutching and just allow that energy to come up and allow it to pass through. And could you let go of your entire aversion to resistance? And just allow that energy to come up. Anything stopping you from saying "yes?" Feel it, and just allow it to pass through.

CHAPTER TWENTY-ONE

THE CHECKBOOK EXERCISE

"If you have a sick body,
you probably have a sick pocketbook--
it's all the same."
--Lester Levenson

We're going to be taking a look at something that really gets in the way of our having abundance. It's very simple, easy to use and is absolutely fabulous in knocking out whatever's in the way of us having abundance--and that's your checkbook. Every time you take your checkbook out and write a check, whether it be a credit card payment, a medical bill, mortgage payment, whatever--if you have a clutching going on, that's exactly what's in the way of you having abundance. It's literally stopping you. And so if you'll feel the clutching, let it go and allow that energy to come up and pass through, you'll open up the flow of abundance.

On top of your checkbook, I suggest you write or paste something there that says, "Release." If you are home, you may want to take your checkbook out and look at the bills you pay on a monthly basis. Either that or you can look at the page of blank checks on the facing page.

Then turn to page 148.

The Check Exercise

Every time we begin to write a check, it's an opportunity to release our resistance to having abundance. Just simply writing a check will show you what's in the way to having total abundance. Sometimes we "clutch" or resist our feelings about the check, thus we can now bring up what's in the way of having abundance from our subconscious thoughts to a conscious level and release those lacking feelings. This is a very powerful way of having abundance fast,

Suggestion: Write the word "Release" on the front of the checkbook to remind you to release feelings of lack or resistance, Don't send the check until you feel 100% released on it and the people you are sending the check to. If you do this consistently, you will be eliminating what you don't want in your mind and be left with what you do want: abundance. Doing this is certain to lead to vast abundance Try it! You'll like it!

		127
		91-2/1221
		_____ 2003
Pay to the order of _____		$_____
_____		DOLLARS
BANK **1** ONE		
		_____

		128
		91-2/1221
		_____ 2003
Pay to the order of _____		$_____
_____		DOLLARS
BANK **1** ONE		
		_____

		129
		91-2/1221
		_____ 2003
Pay to the order of _____		$_____
_____		DOLLARS
BANK **1** ONE		
		_____

I want you to imagine writing your mortgage payment or your rent payment. Just close your eyes and see if any clutching comes up with regard to it. See yourself writing this check, the name of the bank, the name of the landlord, and see if there's any clutching that goes on. Does the amount of money involved cause a clutching or resistance in your feeling center? If it does, could you just let go of the clutching? And more. And more. And even more. Now look at the check again. See if there's any remaining resistance or clutching. Put your head down. Feel the energy. It wants to leave. It's not good, it's not bad, it's just passing through. It's phenomenon. And just allow that energy to leave. And more. And more. And more.

If you want to open up the energy to allow yourself to have a greater abundance than you have now, I recommend that you don't send the check until you feel 100% good about it. Just let go of 100% of your resistance and only send it when you're 100% released and OK about it. Remember to just let go of anything in the way. Maybe it's a feeling of "I haven't got enough," "I don't like it," or "It feels funny." Whatever the block is, just allow yourself to feel that energy and allow it to just pass through.

Now think about a credit card payment if that's real for you. See if you have a clutching when you're writing a check or you even cringe at the mere imagination of doing so. And just allow that energy to come up and just allow it to pass through. And more. And even more. Now think of another check you have to write, should write or must write. Put your head down. See if it brings up any resistance, any clutching. Let go of resisting and clutching and just allow that energy to pass through. It wants to leave. And more. And even more. And see how you feel about the check now. See if there's any resistance, any clutching, any feelings of "I haven't got enough," "I shouldn't do it," or any other insecure feelings--a sensation of wanting to be safe. Could you just let go of that lacking feeling? Just allow it to come up and allow it to pass through. And more. And even more. And allow that energy to come up and allow it to pass through. It's not good, it's not bad. Just allow the energy to pass through. And more. And even more.

You may want to stop here. Take out your monthly bills that you have to pay and your checkbook (or the checks included in this chapter). Then just write the checks one at a time. Notice if there's clutching or resistance. If there is, just allow it to leave and just continue to release until you feel 100% good about the check. Then, every time you take the checkbook out, if you have resistance, you can release the "I can't" feelings in your feeling center. That's the energy holding you back from having more abundance. It's right in front of your nose. I suggest that you never send a check until you feel terrific about it, whether it be a lawyer's check or any kind of check to which you harbor resistance. Just sit down and release on it. Then send the check, feeling 100% good about it. This creates a flow and the flow creates momentum in as well as out. Just allow the flow of abundance to come in as well as out. Now take some time to do this check exercise on all of your bills. It's a good idea to get in the habit of using the check exercise on all your bills--every time you have to write a check. If you do, you'll be amazed at how this will increase your abundance with ease. This single exercise alone will move you to courageousness, acceptance, abundance and peace.

THE GOOD AND BAD EXERCISE

Now let's take a look at the subject of good and bad. It's important to release on things that are good and bad. You see, we have many feelings about what's good and what's bad suppressed in our subconscious mind, but we never look at them. For every good, there has to be a bad. Likewise, for every bad, there has to be a good. It's just like the attachments and aversions. By not releasing them, we are continually perpetuating this good and bad energy. Therefore, we continually hold on to resistance with the subject of good or bad. It's a good idea to release on everything so eventually there is no good or bad feeling suppressed in your subconscious mind. Then you're not resisting this energy subconsciously and, therefore, allowing the flow of abundance to come to you easily. It's a fun exercise, too.

If something is good we have a tendency to hold on to it and stop releasing. If something is bad, we suppress it because we don't want to look at it. At this point, we also stop releasing. Doing this exercise will enable you to decide to release all the time.

So follow along with me. What's good? One thing. Could you see that as a wanting of approval, control or safety? Whichever want it brings up, could you just let it go? And what's bad? Does it bring up a wanting of approval, control or safety? Could you let go of whichever want it brings up? And what's bad? Could you let that go? And what's good? Could you see it as a wanting of approval, control or safety? And whichever want it brings up, could you let it go? Now what's bad? See if there's any resistance there, a clutching. And just allow that energy to come up and pass through. It's not good, it's not bad, it's just phenomenon passing through. And what's good? Just allow that energy to pass through. Let go of holding on to it. And what's bad? And just allow that energy to come up and pass through.

If something's good, we're probably going to try to hold on to it and keep that nice feeling. If something's bad, we're going to resist and suppress it--so, either way, you're practicing suppression. That's why it's good to let go of all this stuff and just allow it to pass through. Remember that we are practicing opening up the releasing muscle and making it easier to release. So what's good? Could you let go of whatever energy is stirred up? And what's bad? Could you let it go? And what's good? Could you let it go? And what's bad? Could you let it go? And what's good? Could you let it go? And what's bad? And could you let go of holding on to that? And what's good? And could you let go of holding on to that? And what's bad? And could you let go of holding on to that? And what's good? And could you let go of holding on to that?

At this point, you might want to continue on regarding what's good and what's bad using the "Good and Bad Exercise" worksheet below. You might want to write down what's good and what's bad and just keep letting go, and letting go and letting go.

"GOOD" AND "BAD" EXERCISE

What's good? And can I let it go?

_____

What's bad? And can I let it go?

_____

What's good? And can I let it go?

_____

What's bad? And can I let it go?

_____

What's good? And can I let it go?

_____

What's bad? And can I let it go?

_____

What's good? And can I let it go?

_____

What's bad? And can I let it go?

_____

After completing this exercise, you can continue on.

CHAPTER TWENTY-TWO

GUILT AND HOW TO DUMP IT

"The more we develop love, the more we come in touch with the harmony of the universe, the more delightful our life becomes, the more beautiful, the more everything. It starts a cycle going in which you spin upwards."
Lester Levenson

AVERSION TO GUILT
Stream of Consciousness:
(Just let your mind think of things about the aversion. Write it down and see what you wrote or thought as wanting approval, wanting control, or wanting to be safe or secure and then release the want.)

What do I like about guilt?

_____

_____

_____

_____

What do I dislike about guilt?

_____

_____

_____

_____

1. Imagine always being guilty all the time--you can't stop.

2. Could I let go of my entire aversion to guilt?

Since most people don't like guilt, let's just start with the aversion to guilt.

So what do you like about guilt? Does that bring up a wanting of approval, control or safety? And could you let go of wanting approval, control or safety? And what don't you like about guilt? Does that bring up a wanting of approval, control or safety? And could you let go of any or all of those wants? And what do you like about guilt? Does that bring up a wanting of approval, control or safety? And could you let go of those wants? And what don't you like about guilt? Is that wanting approval, control or safety? And could you let go of any or all of those wants? And what do you like about guilt? Does that bring up a wanting of approval, control or safety? And could you let go of these wants? Just continue on until you have no more likes or dislikes on guilt. Then move on.

And now let's ask the "squeezing the lemon" question. Imagine always being guilty all the time--you can't stop. You're going to be guilty about everything. Put your head down and see if that brings up a clutching, a resistance or an unwanted energy and just allow that energy to come up and just allow it to pass through. It's not good, it's not bad, it's just passing through. Imagine always being guilty all the time. You can't stop. Just allow that energy to come up and allow it to pass through. And more. And even more. Imagine always being guilty all the time. You can't stop. Just allow that energy to come up and allow it to pass through. And one more time. Imagine always being guilty all the time. You can't stop.

Put your head down. Allow that energy to come up--that guilt that wants to leave--and just allow it to pass through. It's not good, it's not bad--it's just phenomenon passing through. And more. And even more. Keep releasing on guilt until you have no more clutching and then move on to the next question.

Could you let go of your entire aversion to guilt? If there's anything stopping you from saying "yes," allow that energy to come up, let go of resisting it and allow it to pass through. And could you let go of your entire aversion to guilt? And if there's any clutching, any resistance to saying "yes," just allow that energy to pass through. Keep releasing until you're 100% clean on it.

ATTACHMENT TO GUILT
Stream of Consciousness:
(Just let your mind think of things about the attachment. Write them down and see what you wrote or thought as wanting approval, wanting control, or wanting to be safe or secure and then release the want.)

What advantage is it to me to be guilty?

_____

_____

_____

What disadvantage is to me to be guilty?

1.Imagine never ever being guilty again. You couldn't do it if you wanted.

2. Could I let go of my entire attachment to guilt?

And now let's look at our attachment to guilt. So what advantage is it for me to be guilty? What advantage is it for you to be guilty? What advantage is it for you to be guilty? Does that bring up a wanting of approval, control or safety? And whichever want that it brings up, could you just let it go? And what disadvantage is it to be guilty? Does that bring up a wanting of approval, control or safety? And whichever want it stirs up, could you just let it go? And what advantage is it to you to be guilty? Does that bring up a wanting of approval, control or safety? And could you let go of those wants? And what disadvantage is it to you to be guilty? Does that bring up a wanting of approval, control or safety? And could you let go of any or all of those wants? Continue on until you have no more advantages or disadvantages on guilt. Then move on.

And now let's ask the "squeezing the lemon" question. Imagine never, ever, ever being able to be guilty again. You couldn't do it if you wanted to. See if that brings up any resistance, any clutching. If it brings up any unwanted energy, just allow that energy to come up and pass through. Imagine never, ever, ever being able to be guilty again. You can't do it even if you want to. If that brings up a clutching, a resistance, an unwanted energy, just allow it to pass through. Put your head down and just let the energy pass through. Put your head down and just let the energy pass through. Imagine never, ever, ever being able to be guilty again. You can't do it. Just allow that energy to come up and allow it to pass through. Keep releasing until you're 100% clean on it, then move on.

Could you let go of your entire attachment to guilt? If that brings up a clutching, a resistance, an unwanted energy, just put your head down, feel the energy and allow it to pass through. Look for the clutching, and let it go. And could you let go of your entire attachment to guilt and whatever energy it brings up? If there's any resistance to saying "yes" 100%, then just let it go.

Holding on to guilt is one of the big factors that stops us from having abundance in life. By holding on to guilt, we just judge ourselves and beat ourselves up, thus stopping the abundance flow. All we need to do is let it go so we can allow things to happen. If you judge yourself to be guilty, you're actually stopping yourself from having things. Most of us are usually suppressing guilt--and it continually comes up and smacks us in the face. So every time guilt comes up, know that it is something from the past. Allow the energy to come up and allow it to pass through, thus opening up the flow without clutching or resistance to life and the good things in it.

Simply CHOOSE to let go of that which is making you uncomfortable. It's just a choice, it's just a decision. Let it go. Why should you allow guilt or any other feeling to make you uncomfortable? Why should this happen, especially since you now have a method of letting go of anything that bothers you? You don't need to figure it out--just let it go. You don't need to understand a splinter. If you have one, you take a pair of tweezers and you just release it. Just relax and allow any energy to pass through. It's not good, it's not bad. And when you're ready, you can go on to the next chapter.

CHAPTER TWENTY-THREE

HOLDING ON AND LETTING GO

"When we love, not only are we happy,
but our whole life is in harmony."
Lester Levenson

ATTACHMENT TO HOLDING ON
Let's take a look at attachment to holding on. If we weren't holding on, we'd be letting go all the time. So it's a good idea to take a look and discriminate as to why we hold on to everything so as to achieve some clarity.

ATTACHMENT TO HOLDING ON
Stream of Consciousness:
(Just let your mind think of things about the attachment. Write them down and see what you wrote or thought as wanting approval, wanting control, or wanting to be safe or secure and then release the want.)

What advantage is it to me to hold on?

_____

_____

What disadvantage is it to me to hold on?

_____

_____

1. Imagine never, ever being able to hold on. (Let go of clutching or resisting the feeling it brings up in your stomach or chest. Keep releasing until there are no more feelings in your stomach or chest.)

2. Could I let go of my entire attachment to holding on? (Keep letting go until you can say "yes" 100% with no clutching or resistance.)

So what advantage is it for you to hold on? Does that bring up a wanting of approval, control or safety? And could you let go of either wanting approval, control or safety? And what disadvantage is it for you to hold on? Does that bring up a wanting of approval, control or safety? And could you let go of wanting approval, control or safety? And what advantage is it for you to hold on?

Does that bring up a wanting of approval, control or safety? And could you let go of either wanting approval, control or safety? And what disadvantage is it for you to hold on? Does that bring up a wanting of approval, control or safety? And could you let go of wanting approval, control or safety? Continue releasing on this topic before moving on to the next question.

Now let's ask the "squeezing the lemon" question. Imagine never, ever, ever being able to hold on again. You couldn't do it if you wanted to. See if that stirs up a clutching, a resisting, an unwanted energy in your stomach or chest area. Put your head down or your hand on your stomach or chest area and allow that energy to pass through. Imagine never, ever, ever being able to hold on again. You couldn't do it if you wanted to. See if that stirs up an unwanted energy and allow that energy to pass through. Imagine never, ever, ever being able to hold on again. You can't do it. See if it brings up a clutching, a resistance, an unwanted energy in your stomach or your chest. Just allow that energy to pass through. Continue releasing until you're clean on the question before moving on.

Could you let go of your entire attachment to holding on? If you're resisting saying "yes," notice if there's an unwanted energy in your stomach or your chest--a clutching, a resistance. Just let go of this unwanted energy.

And could you let go of your entire attachment to holding on? And whatever resistance is there, just continue to let go until you can say "yes" 100%.

AVERSION TO HOLDING ON
Stream of Consciousness:
(Just let your mind think of things about the aversion. Write it down and see what you wrote or thought as wanting approval, wanting control or wanting to be safe or secure and then release the want.)

What do I like about holding on?

_____

_____

What don't I like about holding on?

_____

_____

1. Imagine always holding on to everything and you can't stop. (Keep releasing until there are no more feelings in your stomach or chest.)
2. Could I let go of my entire aversion to holding on? (Keep letting go until you can say "yes" 100% with no clutching or resistance.)

AVERSION TO HOLDING ON

So what do you like about holding on? Does that bring up a wanting of approval, control or safety? And could you let go of either wanting approval, control or safety? And what don't you like about holding on? Does that bring up a wanting of approval, control or safety? And could you let go of either wanting approval, control or safety? And what do you like about holding on? Does that bring up a wanting of approval, control or safety? And could you let go of either wanting approval, control or safety? And what don't you like about holding on? Could you just let it go?

What do you like about holding on? Does that bring up a wanting of approval, control or safety? And could you let go of these wants? Continue letting go until you have no more likes or dislikes with regard to holding on.

And now let's ask the "squeezing the lemon" question. Imagine always holding on to everything. You can't stop. You're going to have to do it for the rest of your life. See if that brings up a clutching, a resistance, an unwanted energy in your stomach or your chest area and just allow it to pass through. It wants to leave. It's not good, it's not bad--it's just energy passing through. Imagine always holding on to everything. You can't stop You're going to have to do it forever. If there's any clutching or resistance, just allow it to leave. You can't stop. Just allow that energy to come up and allow it to pass through. Continue releasing until you are 100% clean on this question and then move on.

Could you let go of your entire aversion to holding on? If there's any resistance to saying "yes" or clutching, just allow that energy to leave. Could you let go of your entire aversion to holding on and just allow the energy to leave? Continue releasing until you can answer the question 100% with no resistance.

ATTACHMENT TO LETTING GO
Stream of Consciousness:
(Just let your mind think of things about the attachment. Write them down and see what you wrote or thought as wanting approval, wanting control, or wanting to be safe or secure and then release the want.)

What do I like about letting go?

_____

_____

What don't I like about letting go?

_____

_____

1. Imagine always having to let go of everything--you can't stop. (Let go of clutching or resisting the feeling it brings up in your stomach or chest. Keep releasing until there are no more feelings in your stomach or chest.)

2. Could I let go of my entire aversion to letting go? (Keep letting go until you can say "yes" 100% with no clutching or resistance.)

And now let's look at the attachment to letting go. What advantage is it for you to let go? Does that bring up a wanting of approval, control or safety? And whichever want that gets stirred up, could you just let it go? And what disadvantage is it for you to let go? Does that bring up a wanting of approval, control or safety? And whichever want that gets stirred up, could you just allow it to leave? And what advantage is it for you to let go? Does that bring up a wanting of approval, control or safety? And could you let go of those wants? And what disadvantage is it for you to let go? Does that bring up a wanting of approval, control or safety? And whichever want that gets stirred up, could you just let it go? Continue releasing until you have no more advantages or disadvantages coming up. Then move on.

And now let's ask the "squeezing the lemon" question. Imagine never, ever being able to let go again. You can't do it. See if that brings up a clutching in your stomach or chest area, a resistance. Just allow it to pass through. It wants to leave. It's not good, it's not bad, it's just energy passing through. Imagine never, ever, ever being able to let go again. You've lost the ability. And whichever energy that brings up, just let it go.

AVERSION TO LETTING GO
Stream of Consciousness:
(Just let your mind think of things about the aversion. Write it down and see what you wrote or thought as wanting approval, wanting control or wanting to be safe and secure and then release the want.)

What do I like about letting go?

_____

_____

What don't I like about letting go?

_____

_____

1. Imagine always having to let go of everything and you can't stop. (Let go of clutching or resisting the feeling it brings up in your stomach or your chest. Keep releasing until there are no more feelings in your stomach or chest.)

2. Could I let go of my entire aversion to letting go? (Keep letting go until you can say "yes" 100% with no clutching or resistance.)

CHAPTER TWENTY-FOUR

SATISFACTION AND HOW TO HAVE IT ALL THE TIME

"Every thought is an affliction. When the thought waves are completely stilled, there are no more afflictions."
Lester Levenson

ATTACHMENT TO SATISFACTION
Stream of Consciousness:
(Just let your mind think of things about the attachment. Write them down and see what you wrote or thought as wanting approval, wanting control, or wanting to be safe or secure and then release the want.)

What advantage is it to me to be satisfied?

_____

_____

What disadvantage is it to me to be satisfied?

_____

_____

1. Imagine never being able to satisfy myself. (Let go of clutching or resisting the feeling it brings up in your stomach or chest. Keep releasing until there are no more feelings in your stomach or chest.)

2. Could I let go of my entire attachment to satisfaction? (Keep letting go until you can say "yes" 100% with no clutching or resistance.)

"I can't get no satisfaction, I can't get no satisfaction,
And I try, And I try, And I try, And I try,
I can't get no...I can't get no...Satisfaction."

While thinking of these lyrics from the famous Rolling Stones song, "Satisfaction," think about what advantage is in store for you to be satisfied. Does that bring up a wanting of approval, control or safety? And whichever want that gets stirred up, could you just let it go? And what disadvantage is it for you to be satisfied? Does that bring up a wanting of approval, control or safety? And whichever want that gets stirred up, could you just let it go? Continue releasing until there are no more advantages and disadvantages coming up before moving on.

And now let's ask the "squeezing the lemon" question. Imagine never, ever, ever being able to satisfy yourself. Does that bring up a wanting of approval, control or safety? Does it bring up a clutching? And if so, put your head down and allow that energy to pass through. Imagine never, ever, ever being able to satisfy yourself ever again. Put your head down, let go of clutching, let go of resistance, and just allow that energy to leave.

Imagine never being able to be satisfied again. You can't satisfy yourself. Just put your head down and allow that energy to come up and pass through. Imagine never, ever, ever being able to satisfy yourself again. Put your head down and allow that energy to come up and allow it to pass through. Keep releasing until you have no more clutching on the question, then move on.

And could you let go of your entire attachment to satisfaction? And if there's any resistance to saying "yes," could you let it go? And could you let go of your entire attachment to satisfaction? And if there's any resistance to saying "yes," could you just let it go 100%?

AVERSION TO SATISFACTION
Stream of Consciousness:
(Just let your mind think of things about the aversion. Write it down and see what you wrote or thought as wanting approval, control or safety and security. Then release the want.)

What do I like about being satisfied?

_____

_____

What don't I like about being satisfied?

_____

_____

1. Imagine always being satisfied no matter what. (Let go of clutching or resisting the feeling it brings up in your stomach or chest. Keep releasing until there are no more feelings in your stomach or chest.)

2. Could I let go of my entire aversion to satisfaction? (Keep letting go until you can say "yes" 100% with no clutching or resistance.)

Now let's look at the aversion to satisfaction. What don't you like about being satisfied? Does that bring up a wanting of approval, control or safety? And could you let go of either wanting approval, wanting control or wanting safety? And what do you like about being satisfied? Does that bring up a wanting of approval, control or safety? And could you let go of either wanting approval, control or safety? And what don't you like about being satisfied? Does that bring up a wanting of approval, control or safety? And could you let go of these wants? Keep releasing until there are no more likes or dislikes coming up. Then move on.

Now let's ask the "squeezing the lemon" question with regard to being satisfied. Imagine always being satisfied, no matter what. See if that brings up a resistance or clutching. Does it bring up an unwanted energy in your stomach or chest? If so, just allow that energy to come up and pass through. Likewise, imagine always being satisfied, no matter what. You have no choice. If that brings up a clutching, a resistance, just allow that energy to pass through. Imagine always being satisfied, no matter what. And just allow that energy to come up and pass through. Keep releasing until there is no more clutching or resistance regarding this question. Then move on.

Could you let go of your entire aversion to satisfaction? Any resistance to saying "yes?" If so, just allow that energy to come up and allow it to pass through. Could you let go of your entire aversion to satisfaction? If there's any resistance, just let it go.

ATTACHMENT TO TRUSTING
Stream of Consciousness:
(Just let your mind think of things about the attachment. Write them down and see what you wrote or thought as wanting approval, wanting control, or wanting to be safe or secure and then release the want.)

What advantage is it to me to trust?

_____

_____

What disadvantage is it to me to trust?

_____

_____

1. Imagine never ever being able to trust again. (Let go of clutching or resisting the feeling it brings up in your stomach or chest. Keep releasing until there are no more feelings in your stomach or chest.)

2. Could I let go of my entire attachment to trusting? (Keep letting go until you can say "yes" 100% with no clutching or resistance.)

And now let's look at this attachment to trusting. What advantage is it for you to trust? Does that bring up a wanting of approval, control or safety? And could you let go of either wanting approval, control or safety? And what disadvantage is it for you to trust? Does that bring up a wanting of approval, control or safety? And could you let go of either wanting approval, control or safety? Continue releasing on these questions until there are no more advantages or disadvantages--then move on.

And now let's ask the "squeezing the lemon" question. Imagine never, ever, ever being able to trust again. You can't do it. See if it brings up a resistance or a clutching. Just allow that energy to come up and pass through. Imagine never, ever, ever being able to trust again. You can't do it. And just allow that energy to pass through. Imagine never, ever, ever being able to trust again. You can't do it. You've lost the ability. If there's any clutching or resistance, just allow it to pass through.

And could you let go of your entire attachment to trusting? If there's any resistance to saying "yes," just feel it. Allow it to come up. Invite it up and allow it to pass through. Could you let go of your entire attachment to trusting? And just allow whatever energy there is to pass through.

AVERSION TO TRUSTING
Stream of Consciousness:
(Just let your mind think of things about the aversion. Write it down and see what you wrote or thought as wanting approval, control or safety and security. Then release the want.)

What do I like about trusting?

_____

_____

What don't I like about trusting?

_____

_____

1. Imagine always trusting everybody and everything. (Let go of clutching or resisting the feeling it brings up in your stomach or chest. Keep releasing until there are no more feelings in your stomach or chest.)

2. Could I let go of my entire aversion to trusting. (Keep letting go until you can say "yes" 100% with no clutching or resistance.)

And now let's look at the aversion to trusting. What do you like about trusting? Does that bring up a wanting of approval, wanting of control or a wanting of safety and security? Could you let go of any or all of these wants? And what don't you like about trusting? Does that bring up a wanting of approval, control or safety? And could you let go of these wants? And what do you like about trusting? Does that bring up a wanting of approval, control or safety? And could you let go of any or all of these wants? And what don't you like about trusting? Does that bring up a wanting of approval, control or safety? And could you let go of either wanting approval, control or safety?

Imagine always trusting everybody and everyone all the time. See if that brings up a resistance, a rejecting or clutching and just allow that energy to come up and pass through. Imagine always trusting everybody and everything. Allow it to come up and pass through.

And could you let go of your entire aversion to trusting? If there's any resistance to saying "yes," just let it go. Again: could you let go of your entire aversion to trusting. If there's any resistance to saying "yes," could you just let it go?

You may want to ask yourself the questions on the facing page several times. Remember it's just a measure to see how imperturbable you are since starting The Abundance Course. Don't use it to beat yourself up. Remember it's important to know where you are on the Scale of Action. After all, if you don't know where you are and where you're going, you won't be able to get there. You're just examining yourself and your degree of freedom.

And when you're ready to continue, move on to the next chapter.

CHECK TO SEE HOW YOU ARE DOING

Let's look at some self-growth yardsticks. Just take a check and see where you are on the way to freedom and imperturbability by asking the following questions:

* Am I completely at peace?
* How loving am I?
* Do I love all beings?
* Do I accept the responsibility for whatever happens to me?
* Am I free from desire?
* Do I have no attachments and no aversions?
* Am I free to do or not to do the things that I want or don't want to do?
* Do I grant others their beingness?
* Am I accepting of the world and the people around me?
* Am I accepting of myself?
* Am I completely free from reacting to people's wishes and thoughts?
* Am I disturbed?
* Am I able to express myself clearly, freely and truthfully?
* Am I able to be alone and at peace?
* Is my life simple?

CHAPTER TWENTY-FIVE

CLEARING UP PAST RELATIONSHIPS

"Love is smothered by wrong attitudes. Love is our basic nature and a natural thing. That's why it is so easy. The opposite takes effort. We move away from our natural self, cover it, smother it with concepts of the opposite of love and then, because we're not loving, unloving comes back at us. We feel the greatest when we love."
Lester Levenson

One of the things I've found that gets in the way of us having abundance is some subconscious--or even conscious--feelings about our parents, brothers, sisters, significant others, husbands, wives, etc. Therefore, we're going to do a cleanup series to dig up our subconscious thoughts and just allow them to leave.

CLEANING UP ON YOUR MOTHER

Get the idea of allowing yourself to love your mother fully. Let's do a goal chart: "I Allow Myself to Love My Mother". (List all the feelings you can about your mother and release on them.)

_____

_____

_____

_____

_____

_____

_____

_____

See if each of the items you listed conjures up a feeling or thought. Think of something that maybe she did from the past. Maybe there's something about the way she is now. Maybe it's something she told you to do. See if any or all of these bring up a feeling, a resistance or clutching. Could you let go of that clutching or resisting? Put your head down and notice there may be an unwanted energy. Just allow it to come up and pass through. It wants to leave.

Now think about the list titled "I Allow Myself to Love My Mother." Think of something she did to you or said to you that you don't/didn't like. Did that bring up a wanting of approval, control or safety? And could you let go of either wanting approval, control or safety?

Now see if you have any resistance regarding your mother--the way she is, the way she acts or acted--anything you want to change about her. Do you notice an unwanted energy in your stomach or chest? Put your head down and allow that energy to come up. Let go of resisting it and allow it to pass through. Now think about allowing yourself to love your mother. That doesn't mean you need to do what she wants you to do or what she tells you to do. It means you're becoming imperturbable. You just love her for the way she is, not wanting to change her. In case you haven't noticed, you can't really change her anyway.

If you're resisting, you're experiencing a push. Mothers seem to know all about buttons and how to push them. They can make us feel guilty, frustrated, angry, and so on. Think about something that your mother has done to you that makes you feel guilty. And see if it brings up an unwanted energy in your stomach or chest. Then put your head down and just allow that energy to come up... and then allow it to leave.

When you're thinking about your mother, see if there's any more clutching. Is there any resistance? Think about the way she speaks, something she said to you or what she's telling you to do these days. See if any of those bring up an unwanted energy. And just allow that energy to pass through. And see how you feel about your mother after doing so. See if there's anything you'd like to change. Perhaps it's the way she looks, the way she talks, something she said to you once or the way she acts. Put your head down and see if there's any resistance--then just allow that energy to pass through. It's not good, it's not bad, it's just energy passing through. And think of something that bothers you about your mother. Put your head down and allow that energy to come up and allow it to pass through.

Now see how you feel about your mother. Now, at this point, you might want to stop and continue working on the goal sheet titled "I Allow Myself to Love My Mother." Clean up anything you can think of that bothers you about your mother. Perhaps it's something she once said, something she once did-- something that occurred between the two of you. Whatever it is, just see it as

167

unwanted energy. Put your head down and allow it to come up. Or see it as a wanting of approval, control or safety and just let it go. Continue releasing on the topics you listed until there's nothing left and then move on.

CLEANING UP ON YOUR FATHER

"I Allow Myself to Love My Father". (List all the feelings you can about your father and release on them.)

_____

_____

_____

_____

_____

_____

_____

_____

_____

Now we're going to move on to father. Using the "I Allow Myself to Love My Father" worksheet, list your feelings about him. See if there's anything about him that bothers you--something he did, the way he acts. Maybe he's not here anymore in body. Whatever it is, if there's something you'd like to change about it, put your head down and see if there's an unwanted energy that gets stirred up. Just allow that energy to pass through.

And think about your father: "I allow myself to love my father." See if there's something you'd like to change about him. Maybe there's something that happened between you two. See if you'd still change it. You can't change something that once happened, but you can let go of the way you feel about it by putting your head down and just allowing that energy to come up and pass through. See if you're resisting loving your father or clutching. Allow that energy to just come up and pass through. It's not good, it's not bad, it's just energy. And more --and more.

Lester once said if you are loving, you are the lucky one. Examine that for yourself. When you're loving, you're feeling nice about yourself. So why not let go of anything that's bothering you about anybody else so you can feel good?

Don't do it for them; do it for you.

I allow myself to love my father. Let's see if there's any resistance, any energy left. Put your head down and allow it to just pass through. Now take out the releasing sheet on your father and keep releasing until you only have love for him. Look at "I Allow Myself to Love My Father" and let go of anything that bothers you about him. Don't stop until you only feel 100% loving toward him.

CLEANING UP ON YOUR BROTHER OR SISTER
"I Allow Myself to Love My Brother or Sister". (List all the feelings you can about your brother or sister and release on them.)

_____

_____

_____

_____

_____

_____

_____

_____

And now let's look at your brother or sister. See if anything happened between you. If you have more than one, pick one that you would like to change. Could you let go of wanting to change it--that lacking feeling--and just allow it to pass through? And think of something else that happened between you--something that was said or done. See if you have any resistance. Maybe they're pushing your buttons. Could you just allow that energy to come up and allow it to pass through? And see if there's anything that happened that you'd still like to change. Could you let go of wanting to change it? It's a lacking feeling. Allow that feeling to come up and allow it to pass through. And maybe you think they make you feel a certain way. Don't give away your power. Just put your head down and allow that energy to pass through. Think of something they once said to you that you'd still like to change. Could you allow that energy to come through with ease and let it go?

Now if you have more than one brother or sister, you might want to do a goal chart titled "I Allow Myself to Love My Sister" and release on anything that bothers you about them. The same would apply for any other additional siblings.

"I Allow Myself to Love My... _____ ". (List all the feelings you can about your significant other and release on them.)

And now let's go on to any significant others--a husband, wife, boyfriend, girlfriend or any relationship from the past or present. Pick one of these people to clean up on. Think, "I allow myself to love _____.'" When you think about that, does it bring up a feeling, a clutching, a resistance or a wanting of approval, control or safety? And could you let go of that wanting of approval, control or safety? Think about something they've done in the past or something you'd like to change about them. See if that brings up a clutching or resistance in your stomach or chest. Then allow that energy to come up and pass through. It's not good; it's not bad. It's just energy passing through. Now think of something they said or did. Think of how they act. See if these things bother you. Put your head down and allow that energy to come up and pass through.

"I allow myself to love _____.'" See if that brings up a feeling of wanting approval, control safety. And could you let go of wanting approval, control or safety? "I allow myself to love _____.'" See if that brings up a feeling of wanting approval, control safety. And could you let go of wanting approval, control or safety? "I allow myself to love." See if that brings up a wanting of approval, control or safety. Whichever want it stirs up, could you just allow that wanting--that lacking feeling--to leave? "I allow myself to love." See if that conjures up a wanting of approval, control or safety? And could you let go of any or all of these wants?

"I allow myself to love _____.'" Think of something that happened between you--something they said, the way they are, the way they act, the way they treat you, the way they didn't treat you. If any of those ideas stirs up a wanting of approval, control or safety, could you let go of these wants and allow them to pass through? "I allow myself to love." Does that bring up a wanting of approval, control or safety? And could you let go of wanting approval, control or safety?

At this point you might want to do some individual work on your own. I suggest you clean up anything you have on significant others--husbands, wives, boyfriends, girlfriends, whatever--and just continue with the thought, "I allow myself to love _____.'" Then let go of anything that comes up which bothers you. Sometimes we have a difficult person in our lives and some reticence to release on. At these times, the idea of love can be very uncomfortable. However, keep in mind that love is not being stupid. Don't release your stuff for them; *release your uncomfortable feelings for you.* You're giving away your power by holding on to this unwanted energy in your stomach or chest. After all, it is YOUR energy. It's not theirs! Therefore, it takes a little discrimination on your part, but you can decide "I'm going to release it for me" rather than releasing it for them. WHY SHOULD YOU FEEL BAD WHEN YOU HAVE A TECHNIQUE THAT ALLOWS YOU TO FEEL GOOD ALL THE TIME?

So practice this technique and love_____. Continue the "I allow myself to love _____'" exercise on your own right now. Then move on.

LOVE YOURSELF

Now let's work on "I allow myself to love myself." Does that bring up a clutching or resistance in your stomach or chest? Is there an unwanted energy there? Just allow that energy to come up and allow it to pass through. "I allow myself to love myself." If that brings up an unwanted energy, just allow it to come up and allow it to pass through. It's not good; it's not bad. It's just energy passing through.

Now think of something, one thing, you don't like about yourself. Could you see that as wanting approval, control or safety? And could you let go of either wanting approval, control or safety? Now think of something else you don't like about yourself. Maybe it's something you do--a habit. Does that bring up a wanting of approval, control or safety? And could you let go of those wants? And think of something else you don't like about yourself. Does that bring up an unwanted energy in your stomach or chest? Is there resistance? Is there a clutching? Maybe you're thinking of something you do, the way you speak, the way you look, your physique or a specific body part. Could you see that negative, clutching resistance as wanting approval, control or safety? Now think of something else you don't like about yourself. Maybe it's something you do--a habit. Does that bring up a wanting of approval, control or safety? And could you let go of those wants?

Now think about some interaction you've had with somebody in your life. Maybe it's your mother, for example. Would you like to change that incident? Could you let go of wanting to change what happened and allow it to be something in the past? And think about some interaction you've had with your mother again. Maybe it's wanting approval that's getting stirred up? You want her approval or you want your own approval for the way you behave or have behaved. Whatever gets stirred up, put your head down and just allow that energy to come up and allow it to pass through. Now, anytime during the exercise, you might want to put the book down and work specifically on some areas that bring up unwanted energy. Remember the deeper you dig, the freer you're getting and the more you're opening yourself up to allowing positive things to happen in your life. The more we're moving up the chart of emotions--up to courageousness, acceptance and peace--the closer we're getting to the goal of imperturbability.

Now think of some interaction you have with your father or had with your father--something from the past or present. See if that stirs up a wanting of approval, control or safety. And if so, could you let go of these wants? And think of some other interaction you've had with your father--something that happened, something he did or something you did. If it stirs up a wanting of approval, control or safety, could you let go of any or all of those things? And think of another interaction you've had. See if that stirs up a wanting of approval, control or safety. Could you let go of those wants?

Remember you can close the book at anytime to work by yourself on these topics. And now let's look at a significant other--maybe a past relationship, a husband, a wife or somebody important in your life. Think about a past interaction. See if there's something you want to change, something you should have said or something you would have/could have done. Whatever it stirs up, could you see that as either wanting approval, control or safety? And could you let go of either wanting approval, control or safety? And think of another interaction you've had. See if that stirs up a wanting of approval, control or safety. And could you let go of any or all of these wants?

You may notice that you're getting lighter and lighter as you clean up these areas of your life. I would recommend that you continue this work with regard to partners, bosses, etc.--all kinds of people in your life. In so doing, you can clean up on whatever bothers you about them and, consequently, no longer be bothered about anything pertaining to them or your relationships--past and present--with them.

Remember that the main goal is imperturbability. The idea is to get to a place where nothing and nobody ever bothers you again. And as you've been continuing this work, you'll notice that you've been getting more and more imperturbable. Take a check. Notice your reactions in the world. See how you feel about yourself. Look at the Scale of Action in Chapter Eight and see if you've been moving up the chart. See where you were before you learned how to release. Then notice where you are now. As you continue to let go, you'll notice your continued chart ascent.

Now it's time for you to continue this work on your own. When you're ready, proceed to the next chapter.

CHAPTER TWENTY-SIX

STRENGTHENING YOUR INTENTION
TO HAVE IT ALL

"That which you are seeking is seeking you more so."
--Lester Levenson

In this chapter, I'd like to take a look back. Turn to pages 16-17 and look at the intention(s) you had before starting The Abundance Course. Now see where you are in connection to achieving that intention.

Intention is a very important part of life. Most people's feelings are on automatic. They're not clear about what they're doing. They are reactive rather than being quiet. One of the things I suggest that you get in the habit of doing is the following: Before you go somewhere, sit down and decide an intention. Have an intention to have a good time, to get the order, to have fun. Once you decide on an intention, you take yourself off automatic so you don't get reactive. Therefore, if you go to a party, if you have resistance and part of you feels like you shouldn't go, part of you feels that you have to go, sit down and do an advantage and disadvantage session toward going. Then set an intention for the party. You may decide not to go, but because you released on your feelings, whatever you're going to do will be done to the best of your abilities and you'll have a great time. Most people are playing "A: They lose, B: They lose" in life. They have a feeling they shouldn't go, but if they go because their friend wanted them to go, then they have a bad time (A: You lose). If you decide to go, but you didn't release on the feelings when you get there and have a bad time, then it's a case of B: You lose. This occurs because you aren't clear on the intention.

Have a general intention for your life every day. Before you go to a meeting, before you go on a date and/or before you go to a party, have an intention. If you don't know where you're going, you can't get there. By having intentions, it takes you off automatic and allows you to be clear about which direction you want to go. This reminds me of a story I tell about a pilot:

In order for a pilot to take off from the ground, he makes a decision: "I'm going." It is here that he has the intention to take off. And then he rolls the plane around, pointing it in the direction he's going down the runway. He then takes the throttle and pushes it forward. When the plane has enough momentum, it takes off. If the plane doesn't get enough momentum, it just rolls around on the ground and never takes off--or it might just crash. Either way, the plane goes nowhere.

Most of us just don't have an intention in life. We're on automatic. What intention do you have for your life? Do you want to have abundance? Do you want to have health? Do you want to be happy? Do you want to be in peace? It takes a decision on your part--an intention. Take a look and see how strong your intention about your life is. Do you want to override this noisy mind and have it be quiet and happy all the time? What it takes on your part is to have an intention. What intention have you decided to exercise in all the things you've been practicing? Do you have an intention to let it go or do you have an intention to know about it but do nothing? Be smart. Could you let go of being so smart and allow it to be other than what you think it is? What's a good way of overriding this noisy mind that tells you negative thoughts. Could you let go of being so smart and allow it to be other than what you think it is? It's an excellent way of just neutralizing negative thoughts.

Now let's take a look at The Six Steps on page 56 which are the basis of The Method. It is the summary of all the work we've been doing in this course.

STEP 1: You must want imperturbability or freedom more than you want approval, control and security. If that's off, if you want to control a situation, you're not going to release--you're going to be stuck. So you have to resolve: I must want imperturbability or freedom or the goal more than I want approval, control and security. And then you're leaving yourself open for releasing mode. I also would recommend that you take the six steps and hang them on your refrigerator or on your mirror. Some people reduce it into a small size and put it in their wallet. I've written it in the back of one of my address books so I have it all the time. I've had it for years.

STEP 2: Decide you can do The Method and be imperturbable (or free). It's just a decision. Life is a decision. I'm going to let go. Would you? Could you? When? Now? It's a decision. Could I let it go, would I let it go...and when? Decide you can do The Method and be imperturbable. One of the things that helps you in your decision is to continue to write your gains down. Every time you release, write it down. I was disturbed, I went to a meeting and I got all upset. However, I was able to release on it and calm down instantaneously. I had a lack of clarity. All of a sudden, I released and I got clear. Things like that will help you discriminate and reinforce the decision to be imperturbable and practice The Method. And so I would highly recommend that you continue making goals and writing them down.

STEP 3: See all your feelings culminating into three wants: 1. The want of approval; 2. The want of control; 3. The want of security, safety and/or survival. See that immediately and immediately let go of the want of approval, want of control or the want of security, safety and/or survival.

STEP 4: Make releasing constant. If you stop releasing, the muscle shuts down. You'll go right back into your head. So once you start this momentum, it's like that pilot--heading down the runway. He's got enough momentum. If he doesn't have enough momentum, he won't take off. Instead, he'll just roll around on the ground. So once you continue the releasing and open up the releasing mode, just allow this releasing to continue and don't stop. And continue to release. Make releasing constant.

STEP 5: If you are stuck, let go of wanting to control the stuckness. You put the tube down into the energy and you just let go of clutching, let go of resisting and allow the energy to come up and pass through. That's the way you let go of changing the stuckness. Just create a window. If you can't, then release with the tube. Create a window where you got the energy stuck. It doesn't have to be in your stomach or chest area. Whatever works for you, just let it go.

STEP 6: Each time you release, you are happier and lighter. If you release continually, you will continually be happier and lighter. This step is very important. It's the step that took Lester all the way to total imperturbability. He decided that he wasn't stopping until he got all the goodness of what he was doing. The way he described it: He got so much high energy and so much joy by releasing continually that it became uncomfortable. He had to walk it off in Manhattan for hours at three o'clock in the morning, just letting that energy go. And finally he couldn't stand it anymore. He had so much joy that he took a "look-see" behind it--and there was peace. He let the joy go and fell into this peace--and it never left him.

Now, you keep looking for it. Every time you get high, don't stop. Just say to yourself, "Could it get any better?" Then let it go. And could it get any better? And let it go. And decide you're not stopping until you get all the goodness of what we're doing. This is that profound. Just continue to say, "Could it get any better?" and let it go. That'll take you all the way.

If you hold on to something that's good, you're going to stop releasing. You're going to coast--and you're actually practicing suppression without realizing it. And if something's bad, you're going to stuff it. You already know that. So, keep asking yourself, "Could it get any better?" and just allow the energy to pass through.

Take the Scale of Action chart on page 46. Take a look as to where you're at. Decide where you're at and then ask yourself, "Could it get any better?" Let it go. Watch yourself move up the chart. And then, when you see where you are, ask yourself again, "Could it get any better?" Release and move up. Watch what happens. You'll just keep moving up and up and up and up.

Again, the Six Steps are a key to everything.

CHAPTER TWENTY-SEVEN

GETTING THE MOST FROM YOUR RELEASING

"Letting go of all attachments and aversions is letting go of all your thoughts. Thought and desire are the same."

--Lester Levenson

GETTING THE MOST FROM RELEASING

1. As soon as you awaken in the morning, become aware of what you are feeling. Trace the feeling down to the underlying want--and release.

2. Preview the day and release. Have the Six Steps in front of you.

3. In addition to releasing on the go, set aside time for short releasing breaks during the day.

4. If you begin to get stirred up or stressed, notice this, and release.

5. Have some goals you're releasing on daily. Do attachments and aversions exercises on things and situations in your life.

6. Review the day and release. Have the Six Steps in front of you. Release on:

*Circumstances/events/situations

*People

*Resistance to circumstances/events/situations

*When was wanting control stirred up? Wanting approval? Wanting security?

7. Determine where you could have been more aware today, and where you need to be more aware tomorrow, in order to keep your releasing going even more consistently.

8. Be aware of when you are resisting--and release the feeling of resistance.

9. Review the Six Steps daily. Determine where you were off and what you need to do to get back on track.

10. If you have trouble releasing, see where you're off in the Six Steps. Remember--there are no exceptions!

Now, in more detail, we'll examine the ways to get the most from releasing using each of these ten steps.

1: As soon as you wake in the morning, become aware of what you're feeling. Trace the feeling down to the underlying want and release. Do it as soon as you get up in the morning. Don't automatically begin the routine of your day until you've released.

2: Preview the day and release. Have the Six Steps in front of you. Preview the day--see if you have any concerns, expectations or worries. Look at your attitude about the day and make a general intention for it. Also make some specific intentions. Then just release.

3: In addition to releasing on the go, set aside time for short releasing breaks during the day. Sometimes we push through our stuff. Just stop for a minute and release. Have a special releasing place in your office or home. Have a releasing book with you and just stop every once in a while to release. It takes just a few minutes. That little releasing break will help you get through the day without any stress or pressure. Remember: It's just a feeling!

If you're in a meeting, and you feel you're getting overworked, take a bathroom break. Do whatever you have to do to go to a place where you can get away for a moment to release. Have a coffee break just so you can have some time to release. Then continue with the day's momentum. You can put your hand on your stomach or your chest to remind you to release. People around you won't know what you're doing.

4: If you begin to get stirred up or stressed, notice it immediately and start releasing. Don't sit there clutching and resisting. It takes just a moment to release. Remember Step One: I must want freedom more then I want approval, control or security. That will remind you to release. Then the day will go smoothly. Otherwise, you will experience resistance and the day will drag on.

5: Have some goals you're releasing on daily. I recommend you get a releasing workbook and write goals down on a regular basis--four or five of them daily. And continue to release on these goals until they fall in your lap. And then make some more goals. See how goals can help you accomplish the things you want in life without resistance. When you complete the goal, write down "I completed it." If you haven't completed it and it's not falling in your lap, do advantages and disadvantages of having this goal or ask yourself what's the purpose of why I created this goal not to happen. Then you'll come up with an answer. Then release that.

6: Review the day and release. Have the Six Steps in front of you. Release on circumstances, events, situations, people, resistance to circumstances, events or situations. When was wanting control stirred up? How about wanting approval? Wanting security? This will allow you to sleep much better so you're not continually suppressing or holding on to this stuff. You're un-suppressing it. And that will allow you to have a beautiful night's rest.

7: Determine where you could have been more aware of clutching and resistance today, as well as where you need to be more aware tomorrow, in order to keep releasing going even more consistently.

8: Be aware of when you are resisting releasing. Then release the feeling of resistance or clutching. Look for that clutch and just let it go.

9: Review the Six Steps daily. Determine where you're off on the Six Steps and what you need to do to get back on track.

10: If you have trouble releasing, determine where you're off in the Six Steps. Remember--there are no exceptions!

DAILY REVIEW

A daily review or "clean up" is a powerful process which richly repays the effort invested. The process is most commonly done in the evening, although it can be done at any time during the day. In fact, if you get in the habit of stopping periodically and doing this kind of general cleanup in addition to your regular releasing you will find your improving dramatically.

This is a time to look dispassionately over events and interactions: a meeting or gathering at work or with friends, a talk with a loved one, etc. It is the time to extract from them the learning they contain. Then release any attachments or emotional residue. In many ways, the process is like harvesting the seeds of consciousness. In giving our attention and awareness to the events and their lessons, we gain the nourishment they contain and distill their essential value.

The first step is to relax and allow this process to take place from the standpoint of the observer. Judgment and self-criticism only impede the process.

After you have achieved this state of relaxation, look back over the events of the previous hours and allow certain events or interactions to come into your mind. Notice that these may be events you passed over too rapidly or were incomplete for you. Pay attention to what was left unsaid or undone, as well as any unvoiced agendas or wants which are associated with each. Before you release on these wants, stay present with them for just an instant and see if they have a message or lesson for you. Then identify the want: ask yourself if you could let go of wanting approval, control or security.

Do this process as often as you remember each day. It's a terrific addition to what you are now doing.

FAST STEPS TO FREEDOM
*Get everything only by releasing.
*Practice witnessing things more while releasing.
*Take responsibility for everything.
*Take all your joy from within.
*Be all giving.
*Be yourself

Assignment: Pick one of the Fast Steps to try for yourself. Just focus on it and prove to yourself how the "butt" system will work for you.

ADDED SUGGESTIONS

Lester had many ways to try to help us go free. He created these Fast Steps to Freedom, adding these suggestions for their implementation:

1: Get everything only by releasing. You can practice this by releasing only on the things you want to accomplish in life. Releasing is the highest form of action. The mind will tell you, "Sure, you released on it--but now what do you do?" Don't do anything except release. Get everything only by releasing. You'll discover it's the highest form of action. I know this. Lester knew it. You need to prove it to yourself. Only by experientially doing it, will you prove it to yourself. That's where goals are helpful. Get everything only by releasing.

2: Practice witnessing things more while releasing. In order to witness, you definitely have to let go of all your wanting of approval, control and safety. Just be quiet. Watch what happens. Don't say much. Focus inwardly on your releasing. While you're in conflict, just let the wants go and watch what happens. Any situation will immediately resolve if you totally release. Anything impossible is immediately possible when you completely release on it--and you know you're completely released on it when you just don't give a damn about it.

3: Take responsibility for everything, but don't beat yourself up. Just say to yourself, "Wherein did I cause this to happen?" As soon as you ask, it will come up. Sit quietly and then you can release it. If you did it, you can undo it. If you didn't do it, you're going to have to wait for someone or a set of circumstances to stop. However, if you see that you're the one who's doing it, then you're in a powerful position.

4: Take all your joy from within. If you haven't noticed, that's where the joy is coming from. It's the only place it really comes from. Give yourself approval. And more and more. Take all your joy from within. If you can get that, you'll save yourself years of looking around for joy outside yourself. The search for joy outside oneself is a futile and never-ending one.

5: Be all giving. Just decide to be all giving. That doesn't mean you have to give away the store. Just come from a giving place. Treat others like you want to be treated. Do unto others as you expect others to do unto you, etc.

6: Be yourself. Just be and be and be.

HAPPINESS

Now let's take a look at happiness. Use the following prompts to break down your thoughts.

Choose a Topic: _____

What do I need to be happy regarding this topic?

_____

_____

_____

_____

And can I let go of this?

What do I need to avoid in order to be happy?

_____

_____

_____

_____

And can I let go of this?

Did I completely let go?

What do I need in order to be happy? Does that bring up a wanting of approval, control or safety? Could you let go of either wanting approval, wanting control or wanting safety? And what do I need to avoid in order to be happy? Does that bring up a wanting of approval, control or safety? And could you let them go? What do I need in order to be happy? Does that bring up a wanting of approval, control or safety? Could you let go of either wanting approval, wanting control or wanting safety? And what do I need to avoid in order to be happy? Does that bring up a wanting of approval, control or safety? Could you--would you--let them go? Continue with this exercise until you feel complete with your happiness before moving on.

SEND IN YOUR GAINS
An exercise that is very helpful to you and to my office is to send us your gains. There is a gains sheet in the back of the book. Write down your gains from using this course, as well as your comments. When we receive it, we will put you on our mailing list so you'll be able to receive a newsletter. This periodic

mailing will let you know how others are using the course techniques to have abundance. The newsletter will also give you suggestions and ideas regarding how other graduates are using the course. It will also give you telephone numbers for releasing help nationwide, letting you know about support systems. It also provides information regarding advanced courses being held around the country. These courses are fun because you participate in a live setting with other graduates from your own city. You might want to create a releasing support group for yourself and your friends.

I also recommend having all your friends take the course. I've done that myself and it's wonderful. So every place I go, I find myself surrounded by people who know how to release. And that reminds me to release. Sometimes I might not be releasing, and the fact that I'm with somebody who's not bothered by life's miscellaneous things immediately calms me down and reminds me to release. I highly recommend it. It's a wonderful, wonderful idea. Just get all your friends to learn the Release Technique. And be in touch with other releasers.

Let's continue on. Now I want to take a look at a wonderful exercise that's fabulous and very profound. So just follow me.

What is freedom? Now you give an answer, whatever it is. And then I'll continue to work with you.

So what is freedom?

_____

_____

_____

_____

And if it's even more than that, what is freedom?

_____

_____

_____

_____

And if it's even more than that, what is freedom?

_____

_____

_____

_____

_____

And if it's even more than that, what is freedom?

_____

_____

_____

_____

Continue answering this question repeatedly--as many times as it takes--until you go totally quiet.

And now let's ask another question. What do I have to give up to be all loving?

_____

_____

_____

_____

And whatever that answer is, could you let it go? And what else do I have to give up in order to be all loving?

_____

_____

_____

_____

And whatever that answer is, could you let it go? And what else do I have to give up in order to be all loving?

_____

_____

_____

_____

_____

And whatever that answer is, could you let it go? And what else do I have to give up in order to be all loving?

_____

_____

_____

_____

And whatever that answer is, could you let it go? And what else do I have to give up in order to be all loving? Continue to ask yourself that question until you go totally quiet.

THE MIRROR EXERCISE

I have some homework for you. This evening, sit in front of a mirror. Look at yourself in the mirror and release anything that comes up. Just let go of anything you don't like about what you see--the way you are, the way you look and so on. Most of us never look at ourselves. We're too busy looking away.

Release until you totally love yourself. By doing this, you'll be getting closer and closer to opening up the flow of abundance energy, allowing yourself to have everything you want in life. Just love yourself. That's the goal.

WRITE YOURSELF A LOVE LETTER

Also, as a writing assignment, write yourself a love letter. Sit down and write yourself a love letter. Just allow yourself to just love yourself. Good luck. Allow it to be fun and easy.

CHAPTER TWENTY-EIGHT

SPECIAL RELEASING PROCESSES

"As the mind gets quiet,
first the sense of havingness decreases until a measure
of security is felt. It becomes less necessary to have in order to
be. Then the sense of doership decreases until a further security
is felt in that one is not the real doer, that the real doer is a
high power, that one can actually be with much less doing and
it becomes necessary to do in order to be. Finally, your real Self
that has always been in the background steps in and takes over
and you feel that there is nothing necessary
any more that you must have or do,
that there is no choice but to only be!"

Lester Levenson

RELEASING ON THE MIRROR EXERCISE

See how you feel about the mirror exercise. See if anything got stirred up. If you haven't done the mirror exercise, I strongly suggest that you do it right now. It's highly, highly valuable. And see if anything got stirred up about looking in the mirror. Did it bring up a wanting of approval, control or safety? And could you let go of either wanting approval, control or safety? And see how you feel about having looked in the mirror or looking in the mirror. See if it brings up a clutching, a resistance. Could you put the tube into that energy and just allow it to pass through?

And see if there are any other feelings that got stirred up about looking in the mirror or not looking in the mirror. Does that bring up a wanting of approval, control or safety? And could you let those wants go? And more. And even more. And even more. And see if anything got stirred up about looking in the mirror. Did it bring up a wanting of approval, control or safety? And see how you feel about having looked in the mirror even if you haven't looked. See if it brings up a clutching or resistance. Could you put the tube into that energy and just allow it to pass through? And see if there's any other feelings that got stirred up about looking in the mirror or not looking in the mirror. Does that bring up a wanting of approval, control or safety? And could you let go of wanting approval, control or safety? And more. And more. And even more.

RELEASING ON THE LOVE LETTER

Now see how you feel about the love letter you wrote or didn't write. See if that brought up any feelings--a wanting of approval, control or safety. And could you let go of any or all of those wants? And see if writing a love letter to yourself brings up a clutching, a resistance, and just allow that energy to come up and pass through. It wants to leave. Love is your natural state. Just be yourself. Let go of anything that's blocking you from loving yourself 100%. See if anything got stirred up about loving yourself. Did it bring up a clutching or resistance? Just allow that energy to come up and pass through.

Remember the Chart of Emotions? Well, under Acceptance, the first word that shows up is "abundance." What we've been doing is moving closer and closer toward abundance--loving ourselves--acceptance. And when you're accepting of yourself and loving yourself, you're opening up the flow of abundance. You'll be allowing everything to happen to you with ease. You'll have no resistance. In that place, you're no longer guilty, you're not resisting and you're not clutching. You're just allowing everything good to happen. If you can pick up on that feeling--that energy--and just allow things to happen, you'll find that you won't need to do anything but allow it to happen. If you can, it will happen.

THE SPECIAL CLEANUP

Now we're going to do a special cleanup. This is a cleanup that Lester designed for teachers of the Release Technique to allow them to be released when teaching. I thought it would be valuable for you to have it. It's an excellent way of cleaning up before going to meetings and after meetings, as well as having relationships with people, family and friends. So think of an incident in your life that you've had with someone recently. Maybe it resulted in confrontation. Now get that person's face in your mind. Did that person try to control you? If it brings up a clutching or resistance, then just allow that energy to pass through. Put your head down and allow it to pass through. It wants to leave. Did that person try to control you? See if it brings up a resistance or clutching and just allow that energy to pass through. Remember: Don't release for them, release for you. Why should you feel bad when you have a method for feeling good all the time? Just use it. Did you try to control that person back? Did you? If it brings up an unwanted energy in your stomach or chest--just allow it to pass through.

Do you now grant that person the right to be as they are? If you have any clutching or resistance, just allow that energy to come up and pass through. Remember: Don't do it for them, do it for you. Let the energy go so you can feel good, OK? Did you dislike or disapprove of anything in that person? If it brings up a clutching, a resistance, just allow that energy to pass through. Do you or did you dislike or disapprove of anything in that person? Could you let go of whatever gets stirred up and allow it to leave? Did that person dislike or disapprove of anything in you? Did or does that person dislike or disapprove of anything in you? And if that stirs up a feeling, a clutching, a resistance, just allow it to pass through.

Do you now only have a feeling of love for that person? If there's any resistance or clutching, just allow it to come up. Put your head down and allow that energy to come up and pass through. Do you now have only a feeling of love for that person? Just let go of anything that bothers you about that person. And did that person challenge, oppose or threaten you? If it brings up a clutching, a resistance, just allow that energy to pass through. Put your head down and allow it to come out. Did that person challenge, oppose or threaten you? Just let the energy pass through. And did you challenge, oppose or threaten that person back? If so, could you now let it go? Just let go of clutching and resistance. Allow that energy to leave. It wants to leave. Do you only have a feeling of well-being, safety and trust for that person now? If it brings up a clutching--an internal resistance--just allow it to pass through.

Did you reject, cut off or in any way try to be separate from that person? And if it brings up a clutching or resistance, could you now let it go? And did that person reject, cut off or in any way try to be separate from you? And if it brings up a **resistance,** a clutching, could you just let it go? Did that person reject, cut off or in any way try to be separate from you? Whatever energy gets stirred up, just allow it to pass through. Do you now have only a feeling of "you are me" for that person? If there's any resistance or clutching--any unwanted energy in your stomach or chest--just allow it to pass through.

Now look at the face of this person and feel only love. Do you have a feeling of "you are me" for that person? If there are any other feelings, go back to the beginning and continue to release on this person. You might want to go back to the beginning of this exercise and start the questions again. Would you still like to control the way anything happened in that situation? If so, could you let go of wanting to control it? You can't really change something once it's happened, but you can let go of the way you feel about it. Would you like to control the way your day went? Could you let go of resisting and let it pass through? Would you like approval for the way the day went--or any part of it? And if so, could you let go of wanting approval? Let that lacking feeling go--just allow it to come up and pass through. Would you still like to control anything you did in this incident? And if so, could you let go of wanting to control it? Just allow it to be something in the past and let it go.

Are you wanting any approval for yourself or any of the people involved in that incident? Could you let go of wanting approval--that lacking feeling? Is there still any wanting of survival that got stirred up in this incident? If so, put your head down and just allow that energy to come up. Let go of wanting to survive and/or wanting to be safe. Just let it go. Is there any wanting to be separate from that person? It's that lacking feeling again. Let go of wanting to be separate--just allow it to pass through. See how you feel about that person, situation and/or incident. If there's anything bothering you, just allow it to come up and pass through. You may want to go back to the beginning of this exercise and start again.

AN ACCELARATED SPECIAL RELEASE

The following process has been designed to greatly accelerate your use of the Release Technique. It is made up of a series of questions which can be asked before or after meetings, especially if these are with difficult people. These can also work for gatherings with your family or friends--in fact, any situation that involves interaction with other people.

As you work with these questions, you will see they help you improve your relationships, communicate more effectively, resolve conflicts and incorporate releasing more easily into your life. They will also greatly improve your effectiveness and contribute to the integrity of all your interactions.

There are three groups of questions. Each focuses on a separate want. First control--then approval--then security.

The way to work with these questions is as follows:
*Focus on (visualize) the face of the person you would like to release about.
*Ask yourself one question at a time and allow the question to surface your wants. You may often notice that just asking yourself the question will cause you to spontaneously release the want you are focusing on at the moment.
*The third question in each set is designed to help you see if you are fully released on the want about that individual. Keep asking yourself the first two questions in each set and release whatever is stirred up until you can honestly answer yes to the third question.
*Start with the set of questions on control and say with that set until you grant that person the right to be the way they are. This often is just a decision to release to completion. It is possible to get to this point very quickly if you are open to it.
*Do the same thing with each set of questions in order. You'll know when you are fully released on a person when you can see their face and have only love for them.

CLEANUP QUESTIONS

1. Did that person try to control me?
Did I try to control this person?
Do I now grant this person the right to be as they are?
Repeat these questions until you do.

2. Did I dislike or disapprove of anything in this person?
Did this person dislike or disapprove of anything in me?
Do I have only love feelings for this person?
Repeat these questions until you do.

3. Did this person challenge, oppose or threaten me?
Did I challenge, oppose or threaten this person?
Do I have only a feeling of well-being--a feeling of safety and trust--with this
    person?
Repeat these questions until you do.

Look at the face of each person you are working on and feel only love for
them--only a feeling of "you are me" for that person. If there are any other
feelings, go back to the questions.

CHAPTER TWENTY-NINE

CONCLUSION: BUT IT'S ONLY THE BEGINNING

"Only through growth do we really understand what love is."
Lester Levenson

Even though this is the last chapter and the course is completed, it really isn't. This is only the beginning of you using the Release Technique. You can use the book and the exercises over and over again. They all stand on their own. You can turn to any chapter or any exercise and use it individually, keeping in mind some key points, highlighted here:

THE MORE YOU RELEASE, THE MORE SPONTANEOUS YOUR RELEASING WILL BECOME

As you become more proficient with releasing, don't be surprised if you find yourself releasing spontaneously during situations as they occur. Be on the lookout for how easy your releasing will become the more you use the Release Technique. The more you use your releasing ability, the more you will have a releasing attitude toward stressful situations.

I suggest you review the book again and do the exercises repeatedly. You'll find that you may not have grasped certain releasing techniques the first time around. This technique is very profound. The more you release, the more you will understand what is being taught. It's like peeling an onion--you keep getting closer and closer to the core.

CAN I RELEASE AFTER SOMETHING OCCURS?

Sometimes we get so stirred up that we don't always release on the spot. Don't worry about it; you can always release later. Use every down as an up. This will greatly improve your ability to release.

CAN I RELEASE ON AN EXPECTATION?

It's a good idea to release on expectations or anticipations. Sometimes you can ask yourself, "Can I let go of being so smart and allow it to be other than I think it is?" This will neutralize an anticipation and prevent a self-fulfilling prophecy from taking shape.

KEEP RELEASING UNTIL ALL CLUTCHING IS ELIMINATED

Don't save some negative energy for later. While you still feel it, get rid of all negative energy.

WHAT DO I DO IF I'M OVERWHELMED?

Simply put your head down and pull your shoulders back. Move into coura-geousness and ask the energy to come up--and it will leave. Remember that any release gets rid of the accumulated negative energy, so keep chipping away at it instead of giving up. Do an advantage and disadvantage of being stuck or start releasing on something else so you can open the releasing muscle. You can also call another releasing buddy and ask them to help you release.

Remember that you don't have to put your head down during the time you're with people, but you can put your hand on your stomach or chest area to start releasing. Enjoy this wonderful, wonderful technique. Please let me know how you're doing. Contact me via my company's website at www.releasetechnique.com. I'm truly interested in getting feedback on how the program is working for you. If you have a question or if you're stuck, I'll be happy to point you in the right direction.

CLEANUP ON MOVING TO BEINGNESS

Now let's do a cleanup. Just close your eyes and relax--and see if there's any clutching going on in your stomach or chest. Put your head down and allow the energy to come up and allow it to pass through. Now see if there's any resist-ance. If there is, just allow that energy to come up and pass through. See if there's anything you're trying to figure out. That wanting to figure out is the lack-ing of answer. You're actually instructing your mind not to give you an answer by wanting to figure it out. Could you get in touch with that unwanted energy in your stomach or chest area--that "lacking an answer" feeling? Could you let go of that lacking feeling? Just allow it to pass through. And could you let go of wanting to know what to do about it? And more. And even more. Could you let go of wanting to know any answers? And more. And even more.

Have you been disapproving of yourself? Could you call up that disapproval energy, that beating yourself up energy? It's a habit in all of us. Just call it up. Put your head down and allow it to come up and pass through. And more. And more. And even more. And could you give yourself some approval? Just for the heck of it? No reason necessary. And could you give yourself some more approval? And more. And more. And even more. Notice where the approval comes from. It comes from you. It does not come from outside yourself. So could you give yourself some more approval? And more. And more. And even more. Could it get any better? And could you let go and find out? And could it get any better? And could you let go and find out? And could it get any better? And more. And more.

See if you can bring up some of the wanting to control that lacking feeling of being out of control. Remember: wanting equals lack. Could you let go of wanting to control? And more. And more. And could you bring up some of that

190

wanting control? Could you let it go? Would you let it go? And when? And see if you can bring up some more of that wanting control. It's that lacking feeling. Could you let that lack go from your stomach or chest area? And more. And more. And more. And see if you can bring up some of the wanting of approval--the lie that approval lies outside oneself--the lie that you have to do something to get it from someone else. Could you let go of that lacking feeling? And more. And more. And even more. And could you bring up some of the wanting to be safe and secure? And more. And more. Can you see it's a lacking feeling? And can you bring up some more of that lacking feeling and just allow it to pass through? It's not good, it's not bad. It's just phenomenon passing through. And more. And more. And even more. And even more.

Now see if you have a story--a "poor me" story. Do you have an "I can't get what I want" story or "nobody loves me" story? How about an "I'm a victim" story? Whatever story there is, could you just allow it to come up and allow it to pass through? And more. And more. And even more. And even more. Now see if you have another story you'd like to let go. Whatever the story is, could you allow it to evaporate and dissolve? And more. And even more. And even more. See if you could bring up some of the wanting to be separate. Could you let go of wanting to be separate? And more. And more. And more. Think of something or somebody you want to be separate form. Could you let go of wanting to be separate? And more. And more. And even more.

Now get a picture of your mind, whatever that means to you. Remember the television show "I Dream of Jeannie"? Remember how she would evaporate out of the bottle on command? Can you allow that picture of your mind to evaporate and dissolve? And more. And more. And more. And even more. And get a picture of your body, whatever that means to you. And could you allow that picture of your body to evaporate and dissolve? And more. And more. And even more. And get in touch with that part of you that says, "If I don't do it, I won't get it done. I have to do everything." Could you allow the concept that you have to do anything, the belief that you have to do everything, to evaporate and dissolve? And more. And more. And even more. And could you surrender to beingness? Allow beingness to take care of it. Allow beingness to do it for you. And more. And more. And even more.

And now ask yourself the question: If I'm not my mind and I'm not my body and I'm not my ego, then what am I? Whatever spontaneous answer you get, could you give yourself to that answer? Allow yourself to surrender to it. And more. And more. And more. And even more.

This place that you're in right now speaks to you. And for the purposes of this exercise, let's call it "Quiet." Quiet is very spontaneous. It speaks to us differently than the mind, which analyzes things before it answers you. So just take whatever answer you get.

Let's ask Quiet some questions and take the first answer that comes. From Quiet's point of view, is there such a thing as the past? Just notice your spontaneous answer and take what you get.

From Quiet's point of view, is there such a thing as the future?

From Quiet's point of view, is there such a thing as right?

From Quiet's point of view, is there such a thing as wrong?

From Quiet's point of view, is there such a thing as good?

From Quiet's point of view, is there such a thing as bad?

From Quiet's point of view, is there such a thing as birth?

From Quiet's point of view, is there such a thing as death?

From Quiet's point of view, what do you need to do to make a living?

From Quiet's point of view, what do you need to do to awaken, to be realized, to be free?

See if it's possible for anything negative to happen to you in this place that you're in right now. See if it's possible for you to be destroyed in the place you're in right now. Check and see. And could you give yourself to Quiet even more? Just allow Quiet to take you wherever it's going. It's like sitting in a stream on a raft. And just allow yourself to put your bags down. Allow the stream to take you wherever it's going. And more. And more. And even more.

And could you turn your mind over to Quiet and let it do all the thinking for you? And surrender to it even more. And could you turn your body over to Quiet and let it take care of all your bodily functions? And more. And more. And even more. And could you turn anything you had to do over to Quiet? Just allow Quiet to take care of it. And just rest in this place. And in this place, that's where you can dig up your deepest, most suppressed garbage. It wants to leave, so just let it pass through. Lester said don't release to get high, get high to release. So if you're high right now, now's the time to continue digging. Don't just hold on to that nice feeling. Ask yourself, could it get any better? Let go and find out. Don't just hold on to that nice feeling. Ask yourself, could it get any better? Let go and find out. If you like this exercise, you can call and order the cleanup cassette, which you can use over and over again.

And thank you for joining me. And remember to send in your gains. Take a few days to evaluate your gains and send them to me. We'll put you on our mailing list and you'll be known as a Release Graduate. You'll begin to get our magazine, Release, as well as be eligible for various advanced courses. Remember this course is also available to courses and companies. We would love to come and teach this course in person to a company. We can also tailor the course to your company's needs--or any group, for that matter. If you have a group anywhere in the country, we would love to come teach this to them. How about teaching this to your family?

Please stay in touch and, as Lester always said: "Welcome to the Love Boat."

ACTIVITY LIST
Write down your gains and benefits.

_____

_____

_____

_____

_____

_____

_____

_____

_____

_____

_____

_____

_____

_____

A gain is simply feeling good where you felt bad a moment before. Gains are also the specific results you achieve through releasing. They include the large and small benefits, successes and accomplishments you enjoy day to day by using the Release Technique.

Each time you record your gains in your GAINS SECTION, you validate what you have done to benefit yourself. In addition to being a record of your progress, your gains also remind you to keep using the Release Technique.

There are many categories of gains. The following list provides a sampling of gains categories for your reference:

*Positive changes in behavior and/or attitude
*Greater ease and effectiveness in daily activities
*More effective communications
*Increased problem-solving ability
*Greater flexibility
*More relaxed and confident in action
*Accomplishments
*Insights and realizations
*Completions
*New beginnings
*Acquiring new abilities or skills
*Increase in positive feelings
*Decrease in negative feelings

GAINS AND BENEFITS

Date _____

Gains from the Abundance Course

_____

_____

_____

_____

Name _____

Address _____

City _____

State _____   Zip _____

Phone
_____

Fax
_____

If you need more space, please use a separate piece of paper.

May We Quote You?
* Yes, you have my permission to reprint my above gains.
* You may use only the gains I've checked above.
* Please do not use my gains.
* You may use my name.
* Please do not use my name.

Signature_____

Mail Gains To:
Lawrence Crane Enterprises, Inc., Attn: MORE GAINS, 15101 Rayneta Dr., Sherman Oaks, CA 91403 or e-mail us at www.releasetechnique.com.

THE ABUNDANCE COURSE CANDIDATES
People you would like to share the Release Technique with:
Person   List Actions and/or Feelings and Release

_____

_____

SHARE THE METHOD
Mail list to: Lawrence Crane, 15101 Rayneta Dr., Sherman Oaks, CA 91403 or e-mail us at www.releasetechnique.com.

We are all connected--mom and dad, grandparents, sisters, brothers, aunts, uncles, business associates, dentists, physicians, ministers, lawyers, insurance agents, veterinarians, college and/or high school classmates, nurses, travel agents, church members--everybody.

Most of us know thousands of people during our lifetimes. Just imagine if all of us shared The Abundance Course with a fraction of that number. It is truly the gift of a lifetime. Please list names, addresses and phone numbers of people you think would benefit from this course. We will send them a special information packet with a personalized gift certificate from you.

Date:
Your Name _____
Address _____
City _____ State _____ Zip _____
Phone _____ Fax _____
*I do want you to use my name. *I do not want you to use my name.

Your Name _____
Address _____

RELEASING PROJECTS
CONGRATULATIONS

We have spent this time together preparing you in the use and application of the Release Technique. Now you have all you need to complete the journey you've started on your own.

We truly hope you continue using the Release Technique in all areas of your life. While using it on any topic, you will see that it also affects all other areas of your life. As you achieve greater and greater success and contentment, you are helping not only yourself but those around you--your loved ones, friends, co-workers--even the people you meet on the street. They can sense your inner calmness and notice your ability to experience life more fully. We hope you'll share your wonderful gains with these people and join us in our vision of letting everyone have the Release Technique for their own.

Thank you for participating in the training, and our best wishes for the highest state of Abundance and Imperturbability.

Now that you have completed the Abundance Course, you are considered a Graduate. Send us a copy of your gains sheet and we will send you a catalog with a 10% discount coupon good toward your next purchase of products or seminars! We will also enter your name for a FREE subscription to our quarterly newsletter, Release. Sending us your gains will make you eligible to participate in our nationwide advanced seminars.

We offer the live version of the Basic Course regularly in New York, Boston, Phoenix, Los Angeles, San Francisco and Sedona. Also, you'll be eligible to save $171 on the purchase of the Abundance Course audio cassette series. Read on for further details.

We will also send a qualified instructor anywhere in the United States for a group of 25 people or more who would like the Abundance Course for the first time. We offer comprehensive, customized programs that incorporate The Release Technique for groups, organizations and corporations.

If you would like further information regarding any of the above, call us toll-free at (888) 333-9666.

Send your copy of "Gains Sheet" to:
Lawrence Crane Enterprises, Inc., 15101 Rayneta Dr., Sherman Oaks, CA 91403

You can also send your friends to our website at www.releasetechnique.com.

YOUR PERSONAL RECORD OF BENEFITS FROM THE TRAINING

Following are some of the gains others have reported from the training. Please check off, when they occur, those which you experience and make a brief notation as to details. This will be very helpful to you by encouraging you to continue using "The RELEASE® Technique".

1. Increased productivity on the job.
2. Greater efficiency.
3. More effective communications.
4. Greater clarity of mind.
5. Increased ability to make effective decisions.
6. Greater feeling of security.
7. More self-confidence.
8. Improved concentration.
9. A higher energy level.
10. Increased ability to focus your energy.
11. More constructive thinking and action.
12. Higher motivation in constructive directions.
13. Behavioral changes.
14. Inner calmness in difficult situations.
15. Greater awareness of your own behavior and the underlying feelings which motivate the behavior.
16. Increased insight into the behavior and motives of others.
17. The ability to release feelings which you do not wish to have.
18. Feeling happier.
19. Feeling lighter.
20. Feeling freer.
21. Improved relationships with others.
22. A greater degree of control over your life and happiness.

HERE'S HOW PEOPLE USE "THE RELEASE® TECHNIQUE"
HAVE MORE ABUNDANCE WITH EASE

"The most pronounced, tangible evidence that I'm getting only through using the method is in the monetary aspects of my business. I'm on a commission basis only, and I've earned as much in the first quarter of this year as I did in all of last year."

Karen Brock, Woodland Hills, CA
President, Brock Enterprises

"I took The Release Technique because I was under a lot of business and personal pressure. I find now that I'm more relaxed, easier in all my relationships and making a lot more money with much less effort--working smarter, not harder."

Tom Beyers, Scotsdale, AZ
Senior Vice President, First Federal Mortgage Company

198

"My business has tripled since learning the Abundance Course, yet I'm spending most of my time traveling and having fun all the time. The Technique is so powerful, I've had my entire family learn the Technique. I also got rid of 20 years of asthma. Last month, I made over one million dollars using this Technique."

Jim Whitman, Scotsdale, AZ
Manufacturers Representative

"I have regained my focus on abundance thanks to the Abundance course. Customers are calling me to advertise on my radio show--big time! I recommend it to all who want abundance, riches, success, happiness and health. It really does work."

Jacquie Soloman, Phoenix, AZ
Radio Hostess, KFNX

"I'm excited! I have already made over $7,000 and I am working on a deal now. I expect to triple that--anyone can do it. All that the Abundance course claims is true and then some. I can't imagine everyone not taking this course."

Kathy Shoden, Los Angeles, CA
Sales and Marketing

"I just completed the Abundance course and the basic Release Method Course for the first time last weekend. On the second day, I received an offer for a house I have been trying to sell for three years. Before the course ended, I received three offers on the house. My sales results have been amazing--I've had the biggest month I ever had, and that's just in one week! I can't imagine not wanting to learn The Easy Way."

Gayle Henderson, Scotsdale, AZ
Russ Lyon Realty Co.

HAVE ABUNDANT HEALTH
"I took the Abundance Class to have more financial abundance in my life. Not only did I get that big time, but I had a chronic pain in my jaw for 6 years. I was able to get rid of it the very first evening of the course. My golf has improved, I lowered my score by 14 points in two weeks. This course is worth thousands."

Roger Brunnetti
Marketing Consultant

"I have had a full recovery from a boating accident, since taking the course. I did not have full range of motion in my left arm; I do now and I have been able to stop taking 14 different pills."

Raul Marmol, Claremont, CA

VAST ABUNDANCE IS WITHIN YOU--WHY NOT JOIN IN ON THE FUN?
HEALTH GAINS

"During the second day, I worked on an injured foot that had been bothering me for years. I was wearing a bandage and a sandal. The next day, I was able to wear shoes and it didn't hurt me at all! I'm not angry at anyone, and I like myself more, and I feel joy all the time. Wow!"

Cathryn Willmeng, Phoenix, AZ
Real Estate Appraiser

"I let go of lower back pain I had been suffering with for a long time during the third day of the course. I even took off my back support--WOW, what a course."

Gary Sylvester, San Diego, CA
Telecommunications

BE IN TOTAL CONTROL OF YOUR LIFE

"On Sunday morning (during the course), I woke up with the knowledge that I had found the tools that empower me to take back control of my life, and that's not a goal--that's a fact."

Linda Carella, Los Angeles, CA
V.P. Marketing, Tova Corp.

"Acceptance expanded, trust expanded, love expanded, freedom is and continuously unfolds easily! I also received five checks in the mail yesterday-- and money and joy just keep rolling in. I also have a major art show this week at the Scotsdale Art Center and it just happened with ease."

Monica Martinez, Phoenix, AZ
Artist

"This course helped me bring back the value of more consistent releasing. It has given me the awareness to use the tools I have for releasing with ease. Thank you for putting such a practical spin on the method. My life is so much richer for having use of these tools and Lester's wisdom."

Rosalie Lurie, Los Angeles, CA
Fundraiser

"I no longer judge myself and others. I no longer feel guilty about anything; I love myself and others. I'm experiencing peace and joy more and more. I can't imagine anyone not taking this fabulous course."

Scott Jones, Mission Viejo, CA
Advertising Executive

"I gained the ability to stop being counterproductive in life. I can now erase any attitude of 'I never win.' It enabled me to take control of myself--wow!"

Kathy Mullen, El Segundo, CA
Deputy Sheriff

RID YOURSELF OF FAILURE HABITS

"I actually let go of beating myself up. I hadn't thought it was possible. I feel exhilarated and energetic after years of failure. I have more clarity and peace and improved self-confidence. I have a feeling of 'I can' after years of depression and anxiety. Thank you, Lester and Larry."

Liz Ugalde Fortner, Newhall, CA

"I've taken many classes, but it wasn't until I took the Abundance Course that I really, really got on track. WOW--I really didn't know what I was missing! Abundance is the greatest, and our natural way! Don't miss this opportunity."

Ron Hamady, Los Angeles, CA
Movie Producer

MORE GAINS USING "THE RELEASE® TECHNIQUE"
RID YOURSELF OF FEAR AND GAIN CLARITY

"I unlocked my fear, lack and scarcity feelings that stopped me from having abundance for years. It was powerful and fun and easy. I can't imagine anyone not taking this course--it's a must."

Joseph Harrington, Los Angeles, CA
Psychologist

"My clarity in life improved dramatically. I see where I am and where to go next. My abundance improved just in that one weekend--I wish all could attend."

Craig Davis, Winnetka, CA
School Psychologist

"I had severe anxiety when I would get on the freeway. It was preventing me from having a life. Then I took the Abundance course. On the first day, I dumped the phobia. It was so simple that it was almost hard to believe it could be so easy! I now look at life in such a way that it becomes magical. I recommend it to all."

Lauren Brent, Los Angeles, CA
Esthetician

RID YOURSELF OF WORRY AND SPINNING

"I was able to retire from a job I had for years, and I feel terrific about it! I'm using the 'Butt' system and it works. Thank you, the course is the greatest."

Charles Jones, Washington, DC
Psychotherapist

"I released about worrying about the future. My life really works!"

Bebe Young, Paramount, CA
Businesswoman

"I just completed the Abundance Course. My understanding gets clearer and clearer. My decision process is fantastic, and I'm having fun all the time. My business has tripled, and I'm having more time to do what I want. It's easy --anyone can do it."

Judy Smith Whitman, Scotsdale, AZ
Art Dealer

FEEL LOVE ANYTIME YOU WANT

"These past few weeks have been especially wonderful-- 'Joyous' is the true word. More and more I do see myself as one with everything. Right now, Larry, I feel as if I'm going to explode with joy--and I can't stop laughing! All is well! All should join in on the fun."

Clara Sida-McCoy, Glendale, AZ
Housewife/Secretary

"Thanks, Larry, for your loving support, humor and commitment to others having abundance. I often felt the presence of Lester in the room."

Roxanne Kinegard, San Francisco, CA
Homemaker

"The new work that is being done on abundance is fantastic. I'm just busting with happiness and doing and having what I want all the time."

Cecilia Gallagher, Scottsdale, AZ
Business Developer

"I never thought I could feel this good about myself. I now have a tool I can use each day of my life."

Yvonne Medina, Los Angeles, CA
Client Service Genetics Institute

UNLOCK WHAT'S HOLDING YOU BACK FROM HAVING
TOTAL ABUNDANCE AND JOY IN YOUR LIFE--ONCE AND FOR ALL
LEARN TO TRUST YOURSELF

"By the end of Day 2, I achieved a sense of deep calm. While driving home, I found I wasn't so irritated by other drivers and I remained unperturbed. My boyfriend commented on the youthful, lighter look on my face over dinner."

Kim LaChance, Lawndale, CA
Therapist

"I have been going through books and seminars for so long. This course allowed me to see that life can be without problems. The future is wonderful now."

Pirayeh Shaban, Pasadena, CA
Coordinator

IMPROVE RELATIONSHIPS

"I am able to release my anger at my girlfriend whenever she gets angry/jealous about your relationship. Our relationship has greatly improved in a short time."

Jay Torres, Culver City, CA
Salesman

"My relationship with my children has greatly improved. I am able to handle disgruntled clients without being uptight. I lost my craving for smoking and stopped smoking in the first day of the course."

Thomas Mitchell, Los Angeles, CA
Investment Advisor

"Everything is working for me with ease--my relationships are getting better, my business is exploding with ease, abundance just is and it's easy!"

Shawna Leach-Lugo, Phoenix, AZ
Artist

"I can allow myself to love people for who they are, no matter what."

John Cullen, Lake-In-the-Hills, IL
Contractor

MORE REPORTS FROM THE ABUNDANCE COURSE GRADUATES
DROP UNWANTED HABITS

"A few weeks after learning "The RELEASE® Technique", I completely stopped my chain smoking habit and the craving hasn't come back in 15 years since stopping."

Don Janklow, Westlake Village, CA
President, Janklow & Associates

"I have learned to relax by releasing, and an unexpected gain has been that I no longer have a desire for alcohol--it feels good."

Jack Dimalante, New York

"I lost five pounds during the first week of the course without thinking about it!"

Lloyd Scott, Dallas, TX

"I used this method when I was feeling hunger, and I no longer feel the desire to eat."

Rita Recken, Glandorf, OH

ELIMINATE STRESS

"I connected with the ease of releasing. I simply didn't know how much resistance I had. By Sunday, I had so much energy it was great and after only four hours of sleep. I feel lighter and happier."

Ariana Attie, Los Angeles, CA
Legal Secretary

"Sleeping better than I have in years. I quit taking drugs for my arthritis and feel better without them."

Raymond Hanson, Los Angeles, CA

"The first weekend I discovered my feeling of fatigue could be alleviated, and I drove 200 miles without the sleepiness and feeling of heaviness that so often has plagued me."

Ruth A. Riegel, Chicago, IL

"I had several physical ailments including migraine headaches, diverticulitis, gout and severe hypoglycemia, and the week after taking the course was scheduled for surgery. But with a few days after beginning to release, the surgical condition disappeared and never reappeared. My other physical problems cleared up. I believe these good effects are due to the stress reduction brought about by using the Method."

Dr. David Hawkins, Manhasset, NY
Medical Director, The North Nassau Mental Health Center

"I think it is becoming evident, in my observation, that the techniques learned in the program were beneficial to people who work under the stress and strain that we do in the investment banking industry. I have personally benefited, especially when I ran the New York City Marathon shortly after an illness."

Thomas J. Kitrick, New York
V.P., Training and Development, Goldman, Sachs & Co.

Learn Lester's
No Attachments, No Aversions Course!

New Audio Series

Now on audio, personally recorded by Lester Levenson and Larry Crane

Lester Levenson

This new, exciting and professionally produced twenty-session audio series has all of Lester's material that will help you go all the way and have abundance of everything in life. The perfect way for you to achieve a whole new level in conscious and master your life.

I have kept in contact with many of the graduates who have personally used these audios. THE RESULTS HAVE BEEN PHENOMENAL. The momentum has been wonderful and it's spreading. *IT IS MY INTENT TO HAVE YOU LEARN THESE ADVANCED TECHNIQUES AND FULLY KNOW WHAT LESTER KNOWS.* At the core of this course is the magic Lester brought to the subject of attachments and aversions. I have taken these simple, practical and remarkable tools and created this Abundance Course. By using this audio series, you will eliminate the blocks that are stopping you from having complete freedom in your life. I recently completed a remarkable new audio program that brings Lester's course to you in the comfort and privacy of your own home, or anywhere you play audios.

And, having these audios in your possession is like having an instructor at our beck and call. Anytime you want an instructor to help you, just pop an audio into your player! You will sit back and watch your limitations just fly out. You'll have the opportunity to work on issues that are important to you and

you'll learn more about The Technique as you listen to me guide you through the experience, JUST AS LESTER TAUGHT ME.

Here's What You'll Get

- You'll receive 20 audio sessions of ten "How to do it" Abundance Course audios that will change your life forever.
- You will learn in the privacy of your home how to eliminate any and all of life's burdens and obstacles that are in the way of getting what you truly want in life, fast.
- These 20 audio sessions will take you to a place where you will experience total abundance, peace of mind, health and unlimited happiness.
- You'll discover Lester's secret and discover for yourself why it works for you.
- You'll receive a workbook showing you how to use Lester's *No Attachments, No Aversions Course.*
- Yours *FREE!* Order right now or within the next 5 days and we will give you *THREE FREE BONUS AUDIOs VALUED AT $65.* You'll receive the "In My Own Words" audio in which Lester describes his own personal tips to that natural state he called "happiness with no sorrow." And, as a second bonus, you will receive a special audio called "Will Power." In this audio Lester shares the secret to willing things to happen. The third bonus audio is called "Beingness." It takes you to that place that Lester describes.

Don't forget, the solution is available and it's yours for the taking. I know the difference it will make in your life and what it will mean to your

family and loved ones, too. Lastly, may I ask you something? How quickly and easily would you travel if all the burdens you are carrying were removed from your back?

It's so simple. Can you picture it? I know you can.

If you have any questions please don't hesitate to call me 1-888-333-7703. I truly want to make every effort I can to share with you the way to a life of abundance, peace of mind, health and happiness.

Sincerely,

Larry Crane

Larry Crane

The Abundance Course audio series includes 20 sessions of ten "How to Do It" Abundance Course audios in two beautiful vinyl albums with an accompanying workbook—plus:

Three *FREE* bonus audios. All this is yours for only $199 plus $12.95 U.S. shipping and handling. We are making a limited quantity of this set available to seekers and their friends at this special price. Orders will be filled on a first come first served basis, so order yours today. Call toll-free 1-888-333-7703 or mail a check, made out to Lawrence Crane Enterprises, Inc., to:

Release Technique
15101 Rayneta Drive
Sherman Oaks, CA 91403

Outside the U.S. call:
818-385-0611
From Canada call toll-free:
877-472-3317
Fax: 818-385-0563
Email: releasela@aol.com
or visit our Web site:
www.releaseTechnique.com
All credit cards are accepted.

You Save $199—NOW!

Save $\boxed{over \; \$200}$ *for a limited time*

☐ **Yes!** Please rush me the **Abundance Course** Home Study audio set so I may examine it risk-free for 30 days.

☐ **Yes!** I read THE ABUNDANCE BOOK, so I qualify for the special price of $199. I save **$136** off the regular price of $335.

☐ **Yes!** I also qualify for the **3 free audios**, a **$65** value, mine to keep even if I return the material for a full refund.
(Less shipping and handling, of course.)

☐ Please rush me **audio cassettes**. ☐ Please rush me **CDs**.

☐ Enclosed is $211.95 ($199 plus $12.95 U.S. for shipping and handling)
(Overseas orders $246.95 U.S.—$199 plus $47.95 shipping and handling)
CA residents please add $16.41 (8.25%) sales tax. Total = $228.36
Sorry, we do not accept C.O.D. orders.
Make checks payable to Lawrence Crane Enterprises, Inc.

Total _____   ☐ Check ☐ Visa ☐ MasterCard

Your discount code is AB1.   ☐ Discover ☐ American Express

For fast action, call toll-free (24 hours a day): 1-888-333-7703

Name _____

Address _____City_____State_____Zip_____

Phone (day) _____ (eve.) _____
(In case we need to contact you if there is a question about your order.)

E-mail _____ Occupation _____

Credit Card # _____ Expiration Date _____

Signature _____
Please be sure to check your address carefully and indicate any corrections.

The Release Technique
2800 Crusader Circle, Suite 10, Virginia Beach, VA 23453

DOUBLE GUARANTEE
If I am not convinced that the Abundance Course will work for me I may:
1) Receive Free coaching over the telephone, or 2) Return the course
within 30 days for a prompt refund and still keep the 3 free bonus audios.
(Less shipping and handling, of course.)